Grammar and Usage Workbook

Grade 6

McDougal Littell
A HOUGHTON MIFFLIN COMPANY
Evanston, Illinois • Boston • Dallas

Special Features of the Grammar and Usage Workbook

- It contains a wealth of skill-building exercises in grammar, usage, capitalization, and punctuation.
- Each page focuses on one topic or skill. A brief instructional summary is followed by comprehensive reinforcement exercises.
- Key words and phrases are highlighted for greater clarity and ease of use.
- Each page corresponds to a part in the pupil text for easy reference.
- Grammar lessons are leveled. Form A introduces the skill. Form B extends the skill with more advanced exercises.
- Skills Assessment sheets may be used by the student for self-diagnosis and additional practice or by the teacher as a check for understanding.
- A proofreading practice activity is provided for each Grammar and Usage Handbook.

Printed in the United States of America.

ISBN 0-395-86391-0

5 6 7 8 9 10 – MDO – 02 01 00 99

Contents

Grammar and Usage Handbook

What Is a Sentence?

A **sentence** is a group of words that expresses a complete thought. Every sentence must tell whom or what the sentence is about. It must also tell what happened.

Not a Sentence	The street musician.
Not a Sentence	Plays the saxophone.
Sentence	The street musician plays the saxophone.

Identifying Sentences Read each of the following groups of words. If the words form a complete sentence, write *S* after the sentence. If the words do not form a sentence, write *NS*.

1. The moon behind the clouds.
2. The cars skidded on the slick road.
3. The waves splashed against the rocks.
4. The inside of the treasure chest.
5. Carefully climbed the steep mountain.
6. The patterns on the Navajo blanket.
7. Appears on commercials for gym shoes.
8. The motor hummed.
9. The elephants sprayed water in the clowns' faces.
10. The largest shopping mall in the world.
11. The ancient Egyptians probably invented lipstick.
12. Raced across the finish line.
13. Frisbees flew across the park.
14. A collection of toys from a hundred years ago.
15. Chattered noisily for hours.
16. The kites swooped gracefully.
17. Quickly strung the beads.
18. A proud peacock at the zoo.
19. Pattered steadily on the rooftop.
20. Clerks answered the customer's questions.

Subjects and Predicates

Every sentence has two parts: the **subject** and the **predicate.** The subject tells *whom* or *what* the sentence is about. The predicate tells what the subject *does* or *did* or what the subject *is* or *was.*

Subject	**Predicate**
The fishing boat	rocked against the pier.
All of the planes	are on time.

Identifying Subjects and Predicates Draw one line under the subject and two lines under the predicate in each sentence below.

Example The bolt of lightning struck the tower.

1. Ducklings followed their mother around the barnyard.
2. The baseball player pitched a no-hitter.
3. Children worked in factories during the 1800s.
4. A double rainbow appeared after the storm.
5. Several planes circled the airport during the fog.
6. Four of my friends wrote a play about monsters from outer space.
7. A colorful kite soared over the trees.
8. Poisonous snakes have sharp, hollow fangs.
9. Joe paddled his canoe through the rough water.
10. The sheriff closed the road because of the blizzard.
11. A synthesizer produces the sounds of many different musical instruments.
12. The ancient Egyptians believed in life after death.
13. Maya Angelou read a poem at the President's inauguration.
14. Brandon collects baseball cards as a hobby.
15. Herds of deer came down to the pond every evening.
16. Don rides wild bulls at rodeos.
17. Tony's ancestors came to the United States from Italy.
18. Sara spiked the volleyball over the net.

Sentence Fragments and Run-on Sentences (I)

A **sentence fragment** is a group of words that does not express a complete thought. Some fragments do not tell what happened, while other fragments do not tell whom or what the sentence is about.

Some women during World War II. (*What happened?*)
Played professional baseball. (*Who is this about?*)

A **run-on sentence** is two or more sentences written as one sentence. Either the end mark is missing at the end of the first complete thought, or a comma is used incorrectly to separate two complete thoughts.

The skydivers jumped their parachutes opened. (*end mark missing*)
The skydivers jumped, their parachutes opened. (*misuse of comma*)
The skydivers jumped. Their parachutes opened. (*correct*)

Identifying Fragments and Run-Ons Label each group of words *S* (sentence), *F* (sentence fragment), or *R* (run-on sentence).

1. A scary science fiction story about computers.

2. The koala is not a bear, it is a marsupial.

3. Napoleon ruled France.

4. Hit a grand-slam home run.

5. The detective found clues fingerprints were on a glass.

6. Exploded in midair.

7. My favorite comic strip in the Sunday newspaper.

8. Ben Nighthorse Campbell became the first Native American senator.

9. The rock star played the electric guitar his fans screamed.

10. Concerned about wildlife and the environment.

11. A strong gust of wind blew, the curtains fluttered.

12. An African myth about Anansi the Spider.

13. Collected medicinal herbs in the rain forest.

14. The president's daughter laughed, she enjoyed the joke.

15. Colorful piñatas hung from the ceiling.

16. The speaker coughed then he tapped the microphone.

Sentence Fragments and Run-on Sentences (II)

Readers find both sentence fragments and run-on sentences difficult to understand. A sentence fragment is confusing because something is left out. To correct a fragment, add a missing subject or a missing predicate.

Fragment People in ancient Egypt. (*missing predicate*)
Fragment Wore gems for good luck. (*missing subject*)
Sentence People in ancient Egypt wore gems for good luck.

A run-on sentence incorrectly joins ideas that should be separated. To correct a run-on, add the proper end mark at the end of the first sentence. Then capitalize the first letter of the second sentence.

Incorrect The bull charged the matador waved his cape.
Incorrect The bull charged, the matador waved his cape.
Correct The bull charged. The matador waved his cape.

Correcting Fragments and Run-ons Add words to make the fragments complete sentences. Rewrite the run-on sentences as separate sentences.

1. Fans flocked the ballpark on the opening day of the season the president threw the first pitch.

____

____

2. The roller coaster at the amusement park.

____

3. Walked four miles during a snowstorm in January.

____

4. Kim reads mysteries her favorite detective is Sherlock Holmes.

____

5. Gave a speech about his views on animal rights.

____

6. Our class visited an ice-cream factory we saw a maze of steel pipes and incredible machines.

____

7. Astronauts on a secret mission to Mars.

____

8. Scott Olson invented in-line skates in 1982, he was only nineteen years old.

____

The Simple Predicate, or Verb

The complete predicate includes all of the words that tell what the subject does or is. The most important part of the complete predicate is the **verb.**

Some verbs tell about an action. They are **action verbs.**

Hail *fell* from the sky. Shelly *rode* her bike to the store.

Other verbs state that something *is.* They are called **state-of-being verbs** or **linking verbs.**

Soccer *is* my favorite sport. The old bridge *looked* dangerous.

Identifying Verbs Draw one line under the complete predicate in each sentence. Then draw two lines under the verb.

Example The werewolf howled at the full moon.

1. The heart is a very strong pump.
2. Roxanne plays in an all-girl rock band.
3. The small sailboat drifted out to sea.
4. The helicopter rescued the lost mountain climbers.
5. The lights on the robot blinked on and off.
6. Some old castles in England supposedly have ghosts.
7. The Cyclops was a mythical giant with one eye.
8. The rusty gate creaked loudly.
9. Cows are sacred animals in India.
10. Emil adopted a cat from the animal shelter.

Writing Verbs Add a vivid action verb to each blank to complete each sentence.

1. The car ________________ down the road.
2. The horror movie ________________ the audience.
3. The player ________________ the ball into the basket.
4. The hungry teens ________________ the pizza.
5. The spy ________________ the secret papers.

The Simple Subject

The most important word in the complete subject is called the **simple subject** of the sentence. Another name for the simple subject is the **subject of the verb.**

To find the subject of the verb, find the verb first. Then ask *who* or *what* before the verb.

> The audience at the rock concert clapped loudly.
> **Verb:** *clapped*
> Who or what *clapped?* the audience
> *Audience* is the subject of *clapped.*

> The huge dog frightened my younger brother.
> **Verb:** *frightened*
> Who or what *frightened?* the dog
> *Dog* is the subject of *frightened.*

Finding Subjects and Verbs In the sentences below, draw one line under the simple subject and two lines under the verb.

Example Wild violets grow on the prairie.

1. In Greek mythology, Zeus is the ruler of the gods.
2. The monster in the fun house glowed in the dark.
3. Native Americans in the Southwest used adobe for houses.
4. The prickly pear cactus produces beautiful flowers.
5. The little people in *The Wizard of Oz* were Munchkins.
6. Alice followed the White Rabbit down the hole.
7. People during the Middle Ages played dominoes.
8. The junkyard was full of rusty old car parts.
9. Young boys served as soldiers during the Civil War.
10. A camera from the satellite photographed the earth's surface.
11. A coal miner's helmet has a small light above the bill.
12. Political cartoons in the newspapers often poke fun at the government.
13. Bacteria turn milk into yogurt.
14. The reporter interviewed victims of the hurricane.
15. A prism separates white light into the colors of the spectrum.

The Subject in Different Positions

The subject is usually near the beginning of a sentence, before the verb. Sometimes, however, the subject follows the verb. To find the subject in sentences with unusual word order, first find the verb. Then ask *who* or *what* before the verb.

> Into the water dived the swimmer.
> **Verb:** *dived*
> Who or what *dived?* the swimmer
> *Swimmer* is the subject of *dived.*

The subject usually follows the verb in sentences that begin with the word *here* or *there.*

> Here are the keys to the house.
> **Verb:** *are*
> Who or what *are?* the keys
> *Keys* is the subject of *are.*

Putting the subject in different positions adds variety to sentences.

Finding the Subjects in Different Positions In the sentences below, draw one line under the subject and two lines under the verb.

Example Here is your invitation to the party.

1. In the newspaper is a story about a twelve-year-old hero.
2. Near the top of the tree is a robin's nest.
3. Here are the new uniforms for the soccer team.
4. There are over a hundred pieces in this jigsaw puzzle.
5. In Chinese and Japanese stories, dragons usually are friendly creatures.
6. Along the shoreline are flocks of sea birds.
7. Here is a list of the best pizza parlors.
8. From the top of the Sears Tower, Al saw the skyline of Chicago.
9. Over there are new tires for the mountain bike.
10. In northern Scotland, some people spotted the Loch Ness monster.
11. At night the rain pounded on the roof like a drum.
12. Beside the entrance to the subway was a little box-sized newsstand.
13. All of a sudden Marta heard footsteps in the hallway.
14. There were no signs of life on the planet.
15. After school Reggie performed incredible stunts on his skateboard.

Four Kinds of Sentences

There are four kinds of sentences. Each kind needs a specific end punctuation.

1. **A *declarative sentence* tells or states something. It ends with a period** *(.)*.

   Robin wrote about her trip.

2. **An *interrogative sentence* asks a question. It ends with a question mark** *(?)*.

   Which book did you read?

3. **An *imperative sentence* makes a request or gives an order. It usually ends with a period** *(.)*.

   Draw a map of your neighborhood.

4. **An *exclamatory sentence* expresses strong feelings such as joy, surprise, or anger. It ends with an exclamation point (!).**

   How fast the jetliner flies!

Identifying Sentences Label each of the following sentences by writing *D* for declarative, *INT* for interrogative, *IMP* for imperative, or *E* for exclamatory. Add the correct punctuation to the sentence.

1. ____________ The earth orbits around the sun

2. ____________ Are you a stargazer

3. ____________ Look at the stars on a clear, dark night

4. ____________ How brightly the stars shine

5. ____________ Can you find the Milky Way

6. ____________ What a powerful telescope this is

7. ____________ Look at the Big Dipper

8. ____________ Astronomers study the moon, sun, and planets

9. ____________ Copernicus was a famous Polish astronomer

10. ____________ Imagine life on other planets

11. ____________ Is that bright object a flying saucer

12. ____________ Spaceships from Mars invade New York

13. ____________ Do the movements of the planets affect your life

14. ____________ Many people believe in astrology

15. ____________ Read your horoscope in today's newspaper

Finding Subjects in Different Types of Sentences

Interrogative, exclamatory, and imperative sentences may all have unusual word order. To find the subject of an interrogative or exclamatory sentence, change it to a declarative sentence. Then find the verb and ask *who* or *what* before it.

Interrogative Sentence	Are some insects helpful?
Declarative	Some insects are helpful.
Verb	are
	What *are?* insects
	Insects is the subject of the verb *are.*

Most imperative sentences appear to have no subject. In the following sentences, *you* is understood to be the subject.

(You) Close the door.   (You) Brush the dog.

Finding Subjects In the sentences below, draw a line under the subject of the verb. If the subject is understood, write (*You*) after the sentence.

1. Which animals are characters in Aesop's fables?
2. Stay away from the hornets' nest.
3. What a great magic show we saw!
4. There are many myths about the creation of the world.
5. Was that cave dark and spooky!
6. Centuries ago, Roman children played with marbles.
7. Buckle up your safety belt.
8. Where is the key to the bicycle lock?
9. Travel to the future in a time machine.
10. Heroes in comic books have such incredible powers!
11. Draw a map of your neighborhood.
12. In ancient Babylon and Egypt, priests made calendars.

Compound Subjects

When a subject has two or more parts, it is called a **compound subject**. Use compound subjects to combine sentences that repeat similar ideas. The conjunctions *and* and *or* are words used to join compound subjects.

Ana played a video game. Roy played a video game.
Ana and Roy played a video game.

Identifying Compound Subjects Draw two lines under each verb and one line under each part of the compound subject.

1. Erik and I learned a lot from Todd's report on Morocco.
2. The Mediterranean Sea and the Atlantic Ocean border Morocco on the north and west.
3. Highways and railroads connect all of the major Moroccan cities with one another.
4. Farmland, desert, and mountains form the Moroccan landscape.
5. Arabs and Berbers are the two main groups of people.
6. Casablanca or Tangier is the tourists' favorite city.
7. Mining and agriculture are the two main industries.
8. Men and women wear loose-fitting clothes.
9. Couscous or tabouli is common at many meals.
10. Soccer, basketball, and track are the most popular sports.

Sentence Combining Combine each of the following sentence pairs into one sentence.

1. Meg likes stories by Stephen King. Al likes stories by Stephen King.

   ____

2. Maria Tallchief was a famous ballerina. Suzanne Farrell was a famous ballerina. ____

   ____

3. On July 20, 1969, Neil Armstrong walked on the moon. On July 20, 1969, "Buzz" Aldrin walked on the moon. ______________________________

   ____

4. The Brothers Grimm wrote fairy tales. Hans Christian Andersen wrote fairy tales. ____

   ____

Compound Predicates

When a predicate has two or more parts, it is called a **compound predicate.** Use compound predicates to combine sentences with similar ideas.

Tina saved her allowance. Tina bought a new camera.
Tina saved her allowance and bought a new camera.

Identifying Compound Verbs Draw one line under the subject and two lines under each verb of the compound predicate.

1. The Angels scored four runs in the first inning and stayed ahead for the rest of the game.
2. Frederick Douglass escaped from slavery and became a speaker for antislavery groups.
3. King Kong broke loose in New York City, climbed the World Trade Center, and fought off military planes.
4. Stephen Foster taught himself to play the piano at age six and published his first song at age sixteen.
5. Hector came to bat, took three outside pitches, and smashed the fourth one into the stands.

Sentence Combining On a separate sheet of paper rewrite the following paragraph. Use compound subjects and compound predicates to make the writing flow more smoothly.

Everyone pitched in to plan a surprise farewell party for Mrs. Dawson. Janet painted a banner. Sue painted a banner. Kay painted a banner. Three boys collected money. The same three boys bought a present. Scott ordered a big cake. Scott bought other refreshments too. I brought a camera. I hid behind the door. I hoped to get a good picture. When Mrs. Dawson walked into the dark room, we flicked on the lights. We threw confetti. We yelled "Surprise!" That was one of the few times our teacher was speechless.

Linking Grammar and Writing

12
Understanding Sentences

A good story is made up of many kinds of sentences. Here are examples of the four kinds of sentences.

1. My mother is a pediatrician. (declarative)
2. Who is your favorite musical group? (interrogative)
3. Don't forget to feed the baby. (imperative)
4. Watch out for that car! (exclamatory)

Write an example of each type of sentence.

Declarative ______________________________

____

Interrogative ______________________________

____

Imperative ______________________________

____

Exclamatory ______________________________

____

Choose one of the topic sentences below or make up one of your own. Then write a story on a separate sheet of paper. Use all four types of sentences in your story. Vary your sentence patterns so that in a few of the sentences, the subject appears after the verb.

1. Today was the most exhausting day of my life.
2. The Olympic Games are always fun to watch.
3. Everyone needs a special place to be alone.
4. By talking to senior citizens, you can hear many interesting stories.
5. Pets can do amazing tricks.
6. I enjoy reading bumper stickers.
7. Some people have no sense of humor.
8. Learning a new game is challenging.
9. Everybody should have a goal.
10. Around the world, people celebrate holidays.
11. Commercials can be entertaining.
12. Shopping malls are everywhere.

Additional Practice: Understanding Sentences (I)

Identifying Sentences Label each group of words *S* for sentence or *NS* for not a sentence. Add the correct punctuation to each complete sentence.

1. The seaplane revved up its engines
2. Are dragons the relatives of dinosaurs
3. Incredible fireworks on the Fourth of July
4. Call 911 in case of an emergency
5. What a funny comedy show I saw
6. Wrote a letter to the editor about toy guns
7. Where are the mummies in the Natural History Museum
8. Take these old newspapers to the recycling center
9. Armor protected knights in battle
10. How tall that basketball player is

Identifying Complete Subjects and Predicates Label the italicized words in the following sentences *S* for subject or *P* for predicate.

1. Dian Fossey *studied gorillas in Africa.*
2. *Early people* made medicines from plants and berries.
3. The teddy bear *got its name from President Theodore Roosevelt.*
4. In the snow there were *giant footprints.*
5. The Chinese *painted letters with a fine brush.*
6. *The contestants on the game show* seem nervous.
7. The International Whaling Commission *met in Tokyo.*
8. *Gothic novels* have always been popular.
9. *Hundreds of quilters* exhibited their work.
10. Latin *is the source of many words in English.*
11. Clouds of ash *rose upward from the volcano.*
12. On the subway wall there is *a lovely mural.*

Additional Practice: Understanding Sentences (II)

Finding the Verb and Its Subject Draw one line under the subject and two lines under the verb. If the subject is understood, write *You* in parentheses.

1. There are many legends about dragons.
2. Write a fan letter to your favorite movie star.
3. How old are the Pyramids in Egypt?
4. Near Chicago is the Brookfield Zoo.
5. Was Dracula a prince in Transylvania?
6. Inside the robot's head was a computer.
7. The TV camera zoomed in for a close-up.
8. On Halloween the town has a scarecrow festival.
9. Compare two brands of gym shoes.
10. How fast jaguars run!

Compound Subjects and Compound Predicates Combine each group of sentences into one sentence by making a compound subject or a compound predicate.

1. At the water show, the dolphin jumped through a hoop. The dolphin performed other tricks. ______________________________

____

2. Frogs live in cool, moist places. Toads live in cool, moist places.

____

3. Out of curiosity, Pandora opened a box. Pandora released all human ills into the world. ______________________________

____

4. The snake crawls on its belly. The snake swallows food whole.

____

5. Ancient Greeks hung signs to advertise their stores. Ancient Romans hung signs to advertise their stores. ______________________________

____

Review: Understanding Sentences

Fragments and Run-ons Label each group of words *S* for sentence, *F* for sentence fragment, or *R* for run-on sentence. Then correct the fragments and run-ons on a separate sheet of paper.

1. Steve won a bubble-gum-blowing contest he blew a seven-inch bubble.
2. The wind whistled.
3. Collected cans of food for the homeless.
4. The toucan is a colorful bird, it is a native of Costa Rica.
5. The spooky house at the edge of town.

Types of Sentences Label each of the following sentences by writing *D* for declarative, *INT* for interrogative, *IMP* for imperative, or *E* for exclamatory. Add the correct punctuation. Then underline the subject once and the verb twice. If the subject is understood, write *You* in parentheses.

1. Wear your helmet and your kneepads
2. On the wall is a mural about peace and harmony
3. Where are the best zoos in the United States
4. How strong the weight lifters are
5. There are bats in that cave

Compound Subjects and Predicates Change each group of words to a complete sentence by adding either a compound subject or a compound predicate.

1. The baseball player ______________________________.
2. ______________________________ headed out to sea.
3. The racehorse ______________________________.
4. ______________________________ are my heroes.
5. Dinosaurs ______________________________.
6. ______________________________ gave stirring speeches.
7. The audience ______________________________.
8. ______________________________ make good pets.

What Are Nouns?

A **noun** is a word that names a person, a place, a thing, or an idea.

Persons	Places	Things	Ideas
Ricky	Grand Canyon	shoelace	courage
teacher	home	calendar	kindness
Dr. King	college	lawn mower	fear
mechanic	forest	map	excitement

In your writing, use specific nouns that make your ideas and descriptions easy to follow.

Identifying Nouns Underline all the nouns in the following sentences.

1. The usher in the theater shined his flashlight on the empty seats.
2. T. S. Eliot wrote a poem about a cat named Macavity.
3. Dr. Martin Luther King, Jr., fought for equality and freedom.
4. Chinese workers helped build the railroads during the 1800s.
5. In the myths of ancient Greece, Cerberus was a watchdog with three heads.
6. To some Native Americans, the buffalo is a symbol of good fortune.
7. Spiders weave webs to catch insects.
8. The pioneers who traveled to California in covered wagons faced many dangers and hardships.

Using Nouns Complete each sentence with precise nouns.

1. ________________ plays ________________ on the weekends.
2. At the art museum, ________________ admired the ________________.
3. The victims of the ________________ were filled with feelings of ________________ and ________________.
4. The space creature from ________________ was as tall as a ________________.

Common and Proper Nouns

A **common noun** is a general name for a person, a place, a thing, or an idea. Common nouns are not capitalized.

A **proper noun** is the name of a particular person, place, thing, or idea. Proper nouns always begin with a capital letter.

Common Nouns	Proper Nouns
team	Dallas Cowboys
school	Boulevard School
building	John Hancock Center
athlete	David Robinson

Finding Proper Nouns In the following sentences, draw one line under each common noun and two lines under each proper noun. Capitalize the proper nouns.

Example Sears Tower is a skyscraper in Chicago, Illinois.

1. Hurricanes hit the coast of florida during august.
2. A French explorer named cadillac founded detroit.
3. Zora neale hurston wrote novels and collected folk tales about african americans.
4. During world war II, many American women worked in factories while the men fought in europe.
5. Batman lives in gotham city.

Writing Proper Nouns For each common noun that is given, write two proper nouns.

1. athlete __________ __________
2. holiday __________ __________
3. magazine __________ __________
4. movie star __________ __________
5. city __________ __________
6. school __________ __________
7. shopping mall __________ __________
8. musician __________ __________

Singular and Plural Nouns (I)

A **singular noun** names one person, place, thing, or idea. A **plural noun** names more than one person, place, thing, or idea.

Here are seven rules for forming plural nouns.

1. **To form the plural of most nouns, just add *-s.***

   cups desks hands fossils

2. **When the singular ends in *s, sh, ch, x,* or *z,* add *-es.***

   addresses dishes churches foxes buzzes

3. **When the singular ends in *o,* add *-s.***

   stereos radios solos pianos

   EXCEPTIONS: For the following nouns ending in *o,* add ***-es:***

   echoes heroes potatoes tomatoes

4. **When the singular noun ends in *y,* with a consonant before it, change the *y* to *i* and add *-es.***

   butterfly–butterflies army–armies diary–diaries

5. **For most nouns ending in *f* or *fe,* add *-s.* For some nouns ending in *f* or *fe,* however, change the *f* to *v* and add *-es.***

   chief–chiefs safe–safes calf–calves shelf–shelves

6. **Some nouns are the same for both singular and plural.**

   deer sheep trout moose bass

7. **Some nouns form their plurals in special ways.**

   child–children man–men mouse–mice

   tooth–teeth goose–geese foot–feet

Forming Plurals Write the plural for each of the following nouns.

1. tooth ______________________

2. trout ______________________

3. box ______________________

4. monkey ______________________

5. banjo ______________________

6. leaf ______________________

7. thief ______________________

8. volcano ______________________

9. match ______________________

10. country ______________________

11. drum ______________________

12. auto ______________________

13. woman ______________________

14. class ______________________

Singular and Plural Nouns (II)

Always check a dictionary when you are unsure about how to form the plural of a word.

Correcting Plural Nouns Rewrite each sentence, correcting all errors in the spelling of plural nouns. (16 errors)

1. The toy submarine was armed with miniature torpedos.

2. In many fairy tales, wolfs are evil creatures.

3. Crocodiles have powerful jaws and sharp tooths.

4. Famous athletes have appeared in music videoes.

5. During the 1800s, Native American chieves signed treatys with the U.S. government.

6. Martin Luther King, Jr.'s Birthday and Washington's Birthday are legal holidayes.

7. The disc jockies hosted a benefit for homeless childs.

8. Mother kangeroos carry their young in pouchs.

9. Mooses are the largest members of the deer family.

10. Tyrannosaurus rex was one of the most savage dinosaures.

Nouns That Show Possession

A **possessive noun** shows ownership. It tells what or to whom another noun belongs. Here are the rules for writing possessive nouns.

1. **To form the possessive of a singular noun, add an apostrophe and *-s.***

   teacher's ideas   Charles's bike   dog's bone

2. **To form the possessive of a plural noun that ends in *s,* simply add an apostrophe after the *s.***

   jockeys' horses   families' homes   farmers' crops

3. **To form the possessive of a plural noun that does not end in *s,* add an apostrophe and an *s.***

   children's museum   women's basketball   deer's enemies

Writing Possessive Forms of Nouns Write the possessive form of each of the nouns that are in italics.

1. *season* greetings ______________
2. *child* imagination ______________
3. *animal* survival ______________
4. *geese* flight ______________
5. *Mexico* festival ______________
6. *woman* secret ______________
7. *author* books ______________
8. *baby* cradle ______________
9. *men* locker room ______________
10. *cat* toy ______________
11. *oxen yoke* ______________
12. *directors* awards ______________
13. *singer* fans ______________
14. *dwarfs cottage* ______________
15. *sheep* wool ______________
16. *cities* problems ______________

Using Possessives Write the possessive form of each noun in parentheses.

1. Ghosts appear in some of (Shakespeare) plays. ______________
2. The (children) treehouse was a secret meeting place. ______________
3. The monster was created in the (scientist) lab. ______________
4. The (elves) magical powers saved the town from disaster. ______________
5. Sherlock (Holmes) assistant was Dr. Watson. ______________

Linking Grammar and Writing: Understanding Nouns

Picture yourself as the first explorer to visit an unknown part of the earth. The place you explore might be a cave, a mountain, a swamp, a rain forest, the ocean floor, or the North Pole. You are keeping a journal of your exploration. Write a paragraph describing all the strange and wondrous things you see. These things may be real or imaginary. Underline all the nouns in your paragraph. Remember to capitalize any proper nouns.

Additional Practice: Understanding Nouns

Finding Common Nouns and Proper Nouns In the following sentences, draw one line under each common noun and two lines under each proper noun. Capitalize the proper nouns.

Example The poet gwendolyn brooks grew up in chicago.

1. Disney world near orlando, florida, has a castle eighteen stories high.
2. Captain kirk and spock are the main characters in *star trek.*
3. Carl stotz founded little league in 1939.
4. The gods and goddesses lived on mount olympus in thessaly, greece.
5. Atlas supported the weight of the heavens on his shoulders.
6. The vietnam veterans memorial includes a wall made of polished black granite.
7. The detective suspected greed was the motive for the crime.
8. Every halloween, the town has an exhibit of unusual scarecrows.
9. The taj mahal is a magnificent building in india.
10. The movie *glory* tells the story of African-American soldiers who fought during the civil war.

Using Plurals and Possessives Rewrite each sentence, correcting all errors in the use of plural and possessive nouns. (10 errors)

1. Cats cradle is a childrens game played with string.

____

2. The sticky substance in a spiders web catches flys and other insects.

____

3. In folk tales, magic gooses lay golden eggs and foxs play tricks on humans.

____

4. Eudora Weltys book of photoes shows how carefully she observes people.

____

5. Football helmets protect player's heads from injurys.

____

Review: Understanding Nouns

Finding Common and Proper Nouns In the following sentences, draw one line under each common noun and two lines under each proper noun. Capitalize the proper nouns.

1. Georgia o'keeffe painted rocks and skulls bleached by the sun.
2. Amelia Earhart flew nonstop across the atlantic ocean.
3. People in the philippines used the yo-yo as both a toy and a weapon.
4. The white house is closed to the public on sundays, mondays, and holidays.
5. Thomas jefferson wrote the declaration of independence.

Forming Plural Nouns Write the plural form for the following nouns.

1. foot ______________________
2. party ______________________
3. mouse ______________________
4. bush ______________________
5. hobby ______________________
6. shelf ______________________
7. radio ______________________
8. dress ______________________
9. holiday ______________________
10. watch ______________________

Writing Possessive Forms Write the correct possessive form of each noun in parentheses.

1. The Confederate (soldiers) ______________ uniforms were gray.
2. The rock (star) ______________ fans screamed during the concert.
3. Susan B. Anthony fought for (women) ______________ right to vote.
4. The (spies) ______________ mission was to crack the secret code.
5. (Columbus) ______________ voyage in 1492 was the first of several journeys he made across the Atlantic.
6. A polar (bear) ______________ white fur blends in with the snow.
7. The markings around a (raccoon) ______________ eyes looks like a (burglar) ______________ mask.
8. The sports section of the newspaper lists baseball (players) ______________ batting averages and (pitchers) ______________ win-loss records.

Kinds of Verbs

Some verbs tell about action. These are called **action verbs**. Sometimes you can see the action.

We *played* volleyball. Tony *collected* dues from each member.

Other verbs tell about action you cannot see.

Joan *knew* the answer to the question. Greg *learns* quickly.

Some verbs do not show action. Instead, they tell that something *is,* or they link the subject with a word or words in the predicate.These verbs are called **state-of-being** or **linking verbs.**

Here are some common linking verbs.

am	was	be	been	become	feel	sound
is	are	were	being	seem	smell	taste

Look at the linking verbs in the following sentences.

July *is* always hot. Those magazines *are* mine.

Identifying Types of Verbs Underline the verb in each of the following sentences. Label each verb *Action* or *Linking.*

______________ **1.** A comet flashed across the sky.

______________ **2.** The desert looked like the surface of the moon.

______________ **3.** The runner darted toward the finish line.

______________ **4.** Butch Cassidy and the Sundance Kid were famous outlaws.

______________ **5.** Compact discs became popular in the 1980s.

______________ **6.** The magician pulled a rabbit out of his hat.

______________ **7.** The medicine tasted bitter.

______________ **8.** Cars skidded on the slick road.

______________ **9.** The train whistle echoed in the distance.

______________ **10.** Beavers build their homes with mud and sticks.

______________ **11.** The town in Ella's dream seemed strange and unfamiliar.

______________ **12.** Hailstones are little balls of ice.

Main Verbs and Helping Verbs

A verb may be one word or a group of words. When there are two or more words that make up the verb, the last word is the **main verb**. The other words are **helping verbs**.

Helping Verb(s)	Main Verb	Verb
is	dancing	is dancing
has	danced	has danced
could have been	dancing	could have been dancing

The helping verb and main verb are sometimes separated by other parts of the sentence.

Can penguins *fly?* Tina *must* not *have heard* the footsteps.

The most common helping verbs are the forms of *be, have,* and *do.*

be—am, is, are, was, were
have—have, has, had
do—do, does, did

Finding Parts of the Verb Underline the verb in each sentence. Then write the parts of the verb in the correct columns. The first one has been done for you.

	Helping Verb(s)	Main Verb
1. Lisa has painted a mural about families.	has	painted
2. Have you ever seen the Lincoln Memorial?		
3. The President can be elected for only two terms.		
4. The red wolf is becoming extinct.		
5. Did you watch the eclipse of the moon?		
6. Have you ever collected baseball cards?		
7. A balloon will be needed for the experiment.		
8. The actors were dressed in animal costumes.		
9. Frankenstein couldn't control his monster.		
10. The plane had been circling the airport for an hour.		

Direct Objects of Verbs

A **direct object** is a noun or pronoun that receives the action of the verb. To find a direct object, first find the verb. Then ask *whom* or *what* after the verb. The word in the sentence that answers *whom* or *what* is the direct object.

Marvin *played* soccer all Saturday morning.

Marvin *played* what? *soccer*

The direct object is *soccer.*

If no word answers the questions *whom* or *what,* there is no direct object.

The fans cheered loudly.

The fans cheered *whom?* The fans cheered *what?*

The sentence has no direct object.

Recognizing Direct Objects In each sentence, draw one line under the verb and two lines under the direct object. Not all sentences will have a direct object.

Example The scuba diver found a shipwreck.

1. The detective finally solved the mystery.
2. The Bureau of the Mint manufactures all coins in the United States.
3. The monkeys climbed the tall trees in the rain forest.
4. The rabbit in *Alice in Wonderland* carries a watch.
5. The electric eel stuns its enemies with an electric shock.
6. Bats often live in attics and caves.
7. Power lines snapped during the vicious storm.
8. Imagine a city under the sea.

Using Direct Objects Add direct objects to complete these sentences.

1. The city workers paved the ________________________ .
2. Ana played ________________________ in the park.
3. During the summer, many people eat ________________________ .
4. The explorers found ________________________ .
5. Bruce plays the ________________________ in a rock band.

Linking Verbs

Linking verbs connect, or link, the subject with a word in the predicate. Words that follow linking verbs and tell something about the subject can be adjectives, nouns, or pronouns. These words are called **predicate words** because they follow the verb and are part of the predicate.

These pickles *taste* sour. (*Sour* is an adjective.)

A goat *became* our team mascot. (*Mascot* is a noun.)

My best friend is *she.* (*She* is a pronoun.)

Do not confuse nouns following predicate words with direct objects of verbs. Predicate words describe or rename the subject.

Finding Linking Verbs In each of the following sentences, underline the linking verb once, and the predicate word twice.

Example The pizza looks delicious.

1. The dingo is a wild dog of Australia.

2. The dodo bird became extinct around 1680.

3. Tarantulas are the largest spiders in the world.

4. The Chimera is an imaginary creature with a lion's head and a snake's tail.

5. The figures of famous people in the wax museum look real.

6. Caterpillars become butterflies.

7. Many foods from Thailand taste very spicy.

8. Violin music sometimes sounds sad.

9. Rock videos are very popular.

10. The special effects in the movie *Batman* look spectacular.

11. Duke Ellington was a great jazz musician.

12. The orphans in Charles Dickens's novels often feel lonely.

13. The spray from skunks smells terrible.

14. The Cheshire Cat's smile seemed mysterious.

15. King Midas was greedy for gold.

Verb Tenses

Different forms of a verb are used to show time. These verbs are called **tenses**. By changing their forms, verbs tell whether the action or state of being takes place in the present, past, or future.

The **present tense** tells about an action or state of being happening now.

I *ride* the bus. I *am* a dancer.

With plural subjects and with the pronouns *I* and *you* the present tense form of most verbs is the same as the base form of the verb. Add *-s* or *-es* to the base form when the subject is singular: *she runs, he goes.*

The **past tense** tells about an action or state of being completed in the past.

I *paddled* the canoe. I *was* a gymnast.

Form the past tense of most verbs by adding *-d* or *-ed* to the base form of the verb: *walk–walked, move–moved.* These are **regular verbs**. Other verbs, called **irregular verbs,** change their spelling to show the past tense: *sing–sang, bring–brought.*

The **future tense** tells about an action or state of being that will happen in the future.

The sun *will shine* tomorrow. I *will hike* for a mile.

Form the future tense by using the helping verbs *will* or *shall* with the present tense form: *sing—will sing, bring—shall bring.*

Recognizing Verb Tenses Underline the verb in each sentence. Label the verb tense *Present, Past, or Future.*

1. Will robots replace factory workers? ____________
2. Blues musician B. B. King calls his guitar Lucille. ____________
3. The Mayas played a game similar to field hockey. ____________
4. The mockingbird imitated the sound of an alarm clock. ____________
5. Rainforests will disappear if the areas are not protected. ____________
6. Great herds of buffalo once roamed the West. ____________
7. Astronauts' spacesuits protect them from heat and cold. ____________
8. Toy soldiers fight giant mice in *The Nutcracker.* ____________
9. Cars of the future will cause less pollution. ____________
10. Some dinosaurs weighed ten times as much as elephants. ____________

The Principal Parts of Verbs

Every verb has many different forms. All of these different forms are made from just three **principal parts:**

Present	Past	Past Participle
walk	walked	(have) walked
score	scored	(have) scored
marry	married	(have) married

The **present** part of the verb is its present tense. Add *-s* or *-es* to form the singular. The present part used with *will* or *shall* forms the future tense.

The **past** part of the verb is its past tense. The spelling of a verb may change if its present form ends in y or a consonant such as *-h, -d, -p,* or *t.*

The **past participle** is always used with a helping verb such as *have.* Here are some examples.

has walked	had walked	will have walked	shall have walked
have walked	was walked	has been walked	should have been walked

Forming Principal Parts of Verbs Write the past and past-participle forms of each of the following verbs. Choose helping verbs to use with the past participles. The first one has been done for you.

Present	Past	Past Participle
1. study	studied	(has) studied
2. promise	________	________
3. shout	________	________
4. toss	________	________
5. invade	________	________
6. flop	________	________
7. protect	________	________
8. describe	________	________
9. laugh	________	________
10. rub	________	________

Irregular Verbs (I)

Irregular verbs have special past forms that are made by changing the spelling of the present form. Remember these rules whenever you use regular or irregular verbs.

1. **The past form of a verb is always used alone without a helping verb.**
2. **The past participle must always be used with a helping verb.**

Here are the principal parts of four common irregular verbs.

Present	Past	Past Participle
begin	began	(have) begun
break	broke	(have) broken
bring	brought	(have) brought
choose	chose	(have) chosen

Using Irregular Verbs Underline the correct form of the irregular verb in parentheses.

1. All the windows in the house were (broke, broken) during the tornado.
2. The baseball game (began, begun) an hour late because of the rain.
3. Bright sunlight (broke, broken) through the clouds.
4. Immigrants have (bring, brought) their customs to the United States.
5. The mystery (began, begun) with the strange disappearance of the mayor.
6. Has a city been (chose, chosen) for the next Olympics?
7. Jackie Joyner-Kersee (broke, broken) several track records.
8. The prince (chose, chosen) Cinderella to be his bride.
9. The rooster had (began, begun) to crow at sunrise.
10. Daryl (bring, brought) the stray cat to the animal shelter.
11. In 1985, Michael Jordan was (chose, chosen) Rookie of the Year by the National Basketball Association.
12. Construction of the Statue of Liberty (began, begun) in 1875.

Irregular Verbs (II)

Here are the principal parts of four other irregular verbs.

Present	Past	Past Participle
come	came	(have) come
do	did	(have) done
drink	drank	(have) drunk
eat	ate	(have) eaten

Using Irregular Verbs Underline the correct form of the irregular verb in parentheses.

1. The Greek gods and goddesses (drank, drunk) nectar.
2. Albert Einstein (came, come) to the United States from Germany.
3. Snow White (ate, eaten) the poisoned apple and fell into a deep sleep.
4. People have (drank, drunk) cola since the late 1870s.
5. The diver (did, done) a triple somersault off the high board.
6. The bear (came, come) out of its den.
7. Louis Pasteur had (did, done) experiments with bacteria.
8. Many words in English have (came, come) from other languages.
9. Have you ever (drank, drunk) Mexican hot chocolate?
10. The survivors of the crash had (ate, eaten) insects and roots to stay alive.
11. The thirsty camel (drank, drunk) about fifty gallons of water in one day.
12. Can you (come, came) to Mario's surprise birthday party?
13. The astronauts (ate, eaten) freeze-dried food during their space flight.
14. The magician (did, done) a card trick and a disappearing act.
15. Noodles are (ate, eaten) throughout the world.
16. The king rewarded the knight who had (did, done) many good deeds.

Irregular Verbs (III)

Here are the principal parts of four other irregular verbs.

Present	**Past**	**Past Participle**
fall	fell	(have) fallen
fly	flew	(have) flown
freeze	froze	(have) frozen
give	gave	(have) given

Using Irregular Verbs Underline the correct form of the irregular verb in parentheses.

1. Benjamin Franklin had (flew, flown) a kite during a thunderstorm.
2. At the fair, prizes were (gave, given) for the best pies and cakes.
3. Some wacky inventors strapped on wings and (flew, flown) off buildings.
4. The explorers in the Arctic had nearly (froze, frozen) to death.
5. Nicknames have been (gave, given) to many famous athletes.
6. Long ago, people (froze, frozen) food in ice houses.
7. The Hindenburg, an airship, exploded and (fell, fallen) from the sky.
8. The library (gave, given) away old magazines and paperback books.
9. Confronted by a wolf, the rabbit (froze, frozen) in its tracks.
10. The princess had (fell, fallen) in love with a toad.
11. Charles Lindbergh (flew, flown) nonstop across the Atlantic Ocean.
12. The ice on the pond had (froze, frozen).
13. During space missions, some astronauts have (fell, fallen) asleep while floating in the air.
14. Leah (gave, given) a speech about holidays around the world.
15. A flock of geese had (flew, flown) south for the winter.
16. During the parade, confetti (fell, fallen) on the floats.

Irregular Verbs (IV)

Here are the principal parts of four other irregular verbs.

Present	Past	Past Participle
go	went	(have) gone
grow	grew	(have) grown
know	knew	(have) known
ride	rode	(have) ridden

Using Irregular Verbs Underline the correct form of the irregular verb in parentheses.

1. Jack's beanstalk (grew, grown) high into the clouds.
2. Texas is (knew, known) as the Lone Star State.
3. The surfers (rode, ridden) the waves in Hawaii.
4. U.S. astronauts (went, gone) to the moon six times from 1969 to 1972.
5. Have you (rode, ridden) the fastest roller coaster at the amusement park?
6. What comic book hero was (knew, known) as the Man of Steel?
7. The explorers had (went, gone) on a journey to the center of the earth.
8. Pinocchio's nose had (grew, grown) longer because he had told a lie.
9. The explorers (rode, ridden) on camels across the desert.
10. Frank L. Baum's book *The Wizard of Oz* (grew, grown) out of his experience of telling stories to his own children.
11. The sheriff and his deputies (went, gone) after the bandits.
12. At the age of five, Mozart (knew, known) how to compose music.
13. The orchids were (grew, grown) in a greenhouse.
14. Pecos Bill (rode, ridden) a cyclone across three states.
15. In the 1800s, thousands of pioneers (went, gone) west in wagon trains.
16. The contestant on the game show (knew, known) the answer to the puzzle.

Irregular Verbs (V)

Here are the principal parts of four other irregular verbs.

Present	Past	Past Participle
run	ran	(have) run
say	said	(have) said
see	saw	(have) seen
speak	spoke	(have) spoken

Using Irregular Verbs Underline the correct form of the irregular verb in parentheses.

1. Dr. Martin Luther King, Jr., (say, said) in a speech, "From every mountainside, let freedom ring."
2. With wings on his hat and feet, Mercury (ran, run) incredibly fast.
3. In the early 1900s, people (saw, seen) silent movies at little theaters called nickelodeons.
4. How many different languages are (spoke, spoken) in Europe?
5. Track star Wilma Rudolph (ran, run) relays in the 1960 Olympics.
6. What have sports reporters (say, said) about athletes' high salaries?
7. Have you ever (saw, seen) a shooting star?
8. Chief Joseph (spoke, spoken) about the unfairness toward Native Americans.
9. Nick had (say, said) his lines in the wrong order.
10. The hare and the tortoise had (ran, run) in a race.
11. Nora (saw, seen) the toy exhibit at the museum.
12. Is French (spoke, spoken) in parts of Canada?
13. For centuries, sailors claimed that they had (saw, seen) sea monsters.
14. Susan B. Anthony had (spoke, spoken) at meetings about women's rights.
15. Charlie Brown has often (say, said), "Good grief."
16. Has a woman ever (ran, run) for president of the United States?

Irregular Verbs (VI)

Here are the principal parts of four other irregular verbs.

Present	Past	Past Participle
steal	stole	(have) stolen
take	took	(have) taken
throw	threw	(have) thrown
write	wrote	(have) written

Using Irregular Verbs Underline the correct form of the irregular verb in parentheses.

1. The spy (stole, stolen) secret formulas from the scientist's lab.
2. Rachel Carson (wrote, written) about the sea and the environment.
3. During the rodeo a cowboy was (threw, thrown) from a wild horse.
4. During the Middle Ages, people (wrote, written) with quill pens.
5. Mathew Brady (took, taken) photographs of soldiers during the Civil War.
6. In Greek mythology, who (stole, stolen) fire from heaven to help humans?
7. In the science fiction story, computers had (took, taken) over the world.
8. The quarterback (threw, thrown) a forty-yard pass.
9. Stephen King has (wrote, written) many thrillers and horror stories.
10. Robin Hood (stole, stolen) from the rich and gave to the poor.
11. After a wedding, rice is often (threw, thrown) at the bride and groom.
12. The scientist (took, taken) a trip in a time machine.
13. A valuable painting had been (stole, stolen) from the art gallery.
14. The pitcher (threw, thrown) two wild pitches in a row.
15. Many pioneers had (wrote, written) about their experiences in diaries.
16. Have you ever (took, taken) care of a pet?

Confusing Pairs of Verbs (I)

Can* and *May *Can* means "to be able to." *May* means "to be allowed to," "to be permitted to," or "to have the possibility of."

Can you lift this weight? *May* I help you?

Let* and *Leave *Let* means "to allow" or "to permit." *Let* is the present, past, and past participle form. *Leave* means "to depart" or "to let stay or let be." Its principal parts are *leave, left, left.*

Let me go to the game. The buses *leave* at noon. *Leave* your books here.

Lie* and *Lay *Lie* means "to recline" or "to rest." Its principal parts are *lie, lay,* and *lain. Lie* does not take a direct object.

Lay means "to put" or "to place." Its principal parts are *lay, laid, laid. Lay* can take a direct object.

I *lie* on the couch at night. Sarah Ann *laid* the package on the table.

Choosing the Correct Verb Underline the correct verb in parentheses.

1. How fast (can, may) cheetahs run?
2. Cinderella (let, left) behind her glass slipper at the ball.
3. (Can, May) we take photographs of the dinosaur skeletons in the museum?
4. The campers were (lying, laying) on the ground and gazing at the stars.
5. Little League (lets, leaves) both boys and girls try out for teams.
6. A Persian rug with beautiful patterns (lay, laid) on the floor.
7. (May, Can) we bring a tape recorder with us to the concert?
8. The grizzly (let, left) huge tracks in the snow.
9. (May, Can) a laser beam cut diamonds?
10. The construction workers (lay, laid) the foundation of the skyscraper.
11. Some places in the United States don't (let, left) people own pit bulls.
12. The fortuneteller (lay, laid) her hands on the crystal ball.

Confusing Pairs of Verbs (II)

Teach and Learn *Teach* means "to show how" or "to explain." Its principal parts are *teach, taught, taught. Learn* means "to understand " or "to gain knowledge." Its principal parts are *learn, learned, learned.*

I will *teach* you a song. You can *learn* easily.

Rise and Raise *Rise* means "to get up" or "to go up." Its principal parts are *rise, rose,* and *risen. Rise* does not take a direct object. Raise means "to lift something up." Its principal parts are *raise, raised,* and *raised. Raise* usually takes a direct object.

The sun *rose* at six. We *raised* the flag.

Sit and Set *Sit* means "to rest." Its principal parts are *sit* and *sat. Sit* does not take a direct object.

Set means "to place" or "to put." *Set* is the present, past, and past participle form. *Set* can take a direct object.

I *sat* on the lounge chair. Please *set* the vase down gently.

Choosing the Correct Verb Underline the correct verb in parentheses.

1. The islands of Hawaii (rose, raised) from volcanoes under the sea.
2. Alice (sat, set) with three odd characters at a tea party.
3. Anne Sullivan Macy (learned, taught) Helen Keller how to speak, read, and write.
4. The movie theaters (rose, raised) the price of tickets.
5. (Set, Sat) the time machine to the year 2010.
6. Astronauts are (learned, taught) to survive in space.
7. The tide is (rising, raising) along the shore.
8. The campers (set, sat) around the fire and listened to ghost stories.
9. *Star Wars* is (set, sat) in a distant galaxy long ago.
10. The animal trainer (teaches, learns) the circus elephants how to dance.
11. Lin (rose, raised) important questions about the future of our planet.
12. The hot-air balloon (rises, raises) above the treetops.
13. King Arthur (learned, taught) about the powers of the magic sword from Merlin the magician.
14. The table in the museum was (set, sat) with silverware from the 1700s.
15. Girls in colonial America (learned, taught) spinning and weaving from their mothers.

Linking Grammar and Writing: Understanding Verbs

Imagine that you are a stuntman or a stuntwoman in Hollywood. You have just finished filming a dangerous scene. Write a letter to your best friend explaining what you did in the scene. Be sure to use plenty of action verbs. Underline each verb in your paragraph. Check to see that all of your verbs are in the past tense.

Dear ______________________,

____

____

____

____

____

____

____

____

____

____

____

____

____

____

____

Your friend,

____

Additional Practice: Understanding Verbs

Kinds of Verbs Underline the verb in each of the following sentences. Label each verb *Action* or *Linking.*

1. In some legends, dragons guarded treasure. ____________
2. "The Night the Ghost Got In" is a story by James Thurber. ____________
3. Cowboys drove herds of cattle across the prairies. ____________
4. Are owls really wise creatures? ____________
5. Grow crystals for your science project. ____________

Verb Tenses Underline the verb in each sentence. Label the verb tense *Present, Past,* or *Future.*

1. How will people travel in the twenty-first century? ____________
2. The train hauled coal from Kentucky. ____________
3. Some mosquitoes carry diseases. ____________
4. The helicopter landed on the roof of the building. ____________
5. What baseball team will win this year's World Series? ____________

Principal Parts of Verbs Write the verb form given in parentheses. Choose helping verbs to use with the past participles.

1. sing (past) ____________
2. flip (past) ____________
3. score (past) ____________
4. fly (past participle) ____________
5. do (past participle) ____________
6. see (past participle) ____________

Confusing Pairs of Verbs Underline the correct verb in parentheses.

1. The sultan (set, sat) on a velvet cushion.
2. Who (taught, learned) Paul Revere to make beautiful silver objects?
3. The conductor (rose, raised) his baton and the orchestra began to play.
4. The city workers (laid, lay) salt on the icy sidewalks and streets.
5. (Let, Leave) the black beans soak in cold water overnight.

Review: Understanding Verbs

Finding the Main Verbs, Helping Verbs, and Direct Objects
Draw one line under the main verbs and helping verbs. Draw two lines under
the direct objects.

1. Children have been playing tag for centuries.
2. The male peacock will fan his tail feathers for his mate.
3. A house wren might build a nest in an old jug.
4. How many people have climbed Mount Everest?
5. Computers can guide the course of missiles.

Finding Linking Verbs and Predicate Words Draw one line under each linking verb and two lines under each predicate word.

1. The sitar is a musical instrument of India.
2. The police detective felt uneasy in the dark, deserted warehouse.
3. Life was difficult for pioneer children and their families.
4. Sometimes the moon seems magical.
5. *McGuffey Readers* were popular schoolbooks during the 1800s.

Using Irregular Verbs Correctly Underline the correct verb in parentheses.

1. The race car (went, gone) around the curve at 150 miles per hour.
2. Alice dreamed that she had (fell, fallen) down a rabbit hole.
3. Pioneer children (did, done) many chores.
4. Mary Shelley (wrote, written) the famous horror story *Frankenstein.*
5. Captain Kirk (say, said), "Beam me up, Scottie."

Using Verbs Correctly Underline the correct verb in parentheses.

1. Yeast causes bread to (rise, raise).
2. In legends grateful fairies have (let, left) money to helpful humans.
3. Many Japanese people (lie, lay) on floor mats.
4. Michael Jordan (can, may) jump incredibly high.
5. Julia Ward Howe wanted to (set, sat) aside a special day to honor mothers.

Skills Assessment 1

Directions One or more of the underlined sections in the following sentences may contain an error in grammar, usage, punctuation, spelling, or capitalization. Write the letter of each incorrect section. Then rewrite the section correctly. If there is no error in an item, write *D.*

Example Gwendolyn Brooks has wrote **A** poems for both adults **B** and children. **C** Have you read her poem "We Real Cool"? No error **D**

Answer **A**—written

1. The first guide dog for the blind in the United States was **A** Buddy, a female German shepherd from Nashville, tennessee. **B** In 1928, she was trained **C** in Switzerland. No error **D**

2. Have you read Aesop's **A** fable about a wolf in sheeps **B** clothing? The moral of the fable has learned **C** me an important lesson. No error **D**

3. Most of Eudora Welty's stories are set **A** in Mississippi, she **B** growed **C** up in this state. No error **D**

4. Strong winds teared **A** the ship's sails and broke **B** its mast. Then the ship sank **C** to the bottom of the ocean. No error **D**

5. The art treasures **A** on exhibit at the museum. Reveal **B** many of the mysterys **C** of ancient Egyptian culture. No error **D**

6. Why does juice rise **A** in a straw? **B** The air pressure outside the straw pushes **C** juice into the straw. No error **D**

7. Felipe had rode **A** an elevator to the fiftieth floor of a skyscraper. Then he felt **B** as though his eardrums **C** were popping. No error **D**

8. The campers set **A** around the campfire and swapped scary stories. **B** Suddenly, they heard the sound of howling wolfs. **C** No error **D**

9. Because of the oil spill, beachs (A) along the shore were damaged. Many birds' (B) feathers (C) were coated with oil, and the birds were unable to fly. No error (D)

10. All of England's knights gone (A) to London for a great jousting tournament. Among them was Arthur he (B) would soon become the king because of his remarkable abilities. (C) No error (D)

11. As a child, the Author (A) Yoshiko Uchida. Wrote (B) stories on brown wrapping (C) paper. No error (D)

12. The detective looked for fingerprints on all the doorknobs (A) but found none. Apparently, the thieves (B) had worn (C) gloves. No error (D)

13. Red foxes (A) are farmers (B) helpers. These animals destroy many pests, such as field mouses. (C) No error (D)

14. The spanish (A) padres were priests. They built (B) a chain of missions in California (C) during the 1700s and 1800s. No error (D)

15. Rita's new sunglasses (A) block out 100 percent of the suns (B) harmful rays. (C) No error (D)

Pronouns and Antecedents

A **pronoun** is used in place of a noun. The word a pronoun stands for is the **antecedent** of the pronoun.

Joan will ask *her* mother for permission.

The pronoun *her* is used in place of the noun *Joan's. Joan* is the antecedent of *her.*

Pronouns can be either singular or plural.

Singular Pronouns			**Plural Pronouns**		
I	my, mine	me	we	our, ours	us
you	your, yours	you	you	your, yours	you
he	his	him	they	their, theirs	them
she	her, hers	her			
it	its	it			

Use a singular pronoun with a singular antecedent. Use a plural pronoun with a plural antecedent. This is called making the pronoun **agree** with its antecedent in number.

The music (singular) began. *It* (singular) was lovely.
People (plural) applauded. *They* (plural) were pleased.

Identifying Pronouns Underline each pronoun in the following sentences. Draw an arrow to the antecedent of the pronoun.

1. Since ancient times, children have worked to help their families.
2. Sally Ride made history when she became the first U.S. woman in space.
3. The sharp quills on the porcupine protect it from its enemies.
4. Paul Bunyan, a giant lumberjack, combed his beard with a pine tree.

Substituting Pronouns for Nouns Rewrite the following sentences. Replace the italicized words with pronouns.

1. Margaret wrote about *Margaret's* pioneer experiences in a diary.

   ____

2. After the spaceship was launched, *the spaceship* exploded in midair.

   ____

3. Arthur and *Arthur's* knights arrived at the beautiful city of Camelot.

   ____

4. Bats hang upside down when *bats* are sleeping.

   ____

Using Subject Pronouns

The following pronouns are **subject pronouns:**

Singular I, you, he, she, it **Plural** we, you, they

Use only subject pronouns as the subjects of verbs. If you are unsure about what pronoun to use in a compound subject, try dividing the compound subject into two parts.

Sandy and (I, me) made pizza. *Sandy* made pizza. *I* made pizza.
Sandy and *I* made pizza.

Use subject pronouns after linking verbs.

The winners were Tom and *she.* The manager is *he.*

Sometimes a subject pronoun is followed by a noun in the subject of a sentence. To help you decide which pronoun to use, leave out the noun.

(We, Us) girls hiked a mile.
We hiked a mile. *Us* hiked a mile.
We girls hiked a mile.

Choosing the Correct Pronoun Underline the correct pronoun in each sentence.

1. Neil Armstrong and (he, him) planted a U.S. flag on the moon.
2. Clarence and (I, me) drew a map of an imaginary island.
3. The ones who defeated the scary monsters were (they, them)!
4. Tina and (she, her) saw an exhibit about garbage at the children's museum.

Using Subject Pronouns Rewrite the second sentence of each pair. Replace the repeated word or words with a subject pronoun.

1. During the Middle Ages, books were very precious. Books were often attached to bookcases with chains.

   ____

2. In Australia, a baby kangaroo has a special name. A baby kangaroo is called a joey.

   ____

3. Thurgood Marshall was the first African-American justice of the Supreme Court of the United States. Thurgood Marshall served from 1967 to 1991.

   ____

4. Bernice and I are ballerinas. Bernice and I performed in *The Nutcracker.*

   ____

Using Object Pronouns

When pronouns are used as objects, they have special forms. These are **object pronouns.**

Singular me, you, him, her, it **Plural** us, you, them

Use these pronouns as objects of verbs and objects of prepositions.

Ms. Banks drove *us* to school. (object of verb)
The rest of the team came with *her.* (object of preposition)

A pronoun is sometimes part of a compound object. If you are not sure which pronoun to use, try dividing the compound object into two parts.

Mary helped (he, him) and (I, me).
Mary helped *him.* Mary helped *me.*
Mary helped *him* and *me.*

Identifying Object Pronouns Underline the correct pronoun in each sentence.

1. Ben described the powwow in Arizona to Victor and (she, her).
2. Sylvia invited you and (I, me) to the jazz festival in Grant Park.
3. The elves hid in the woods, where nobody could find (they, them).
4. The director wants either Sam or (he, him) to play the part of Batman.
5. A huge bear growled at Davy Crockett and began wrestling with (he, him).
6. The teacher told (we, us) about the adventures of Sinbad the Sailor.

Using Object Pronouns Complete each of the following sentences with a correct object pronoun.

1. The matador fanned his cape, and the bull came charging toward

   ________________ .

2. Some animals pretend to be dead when an enemy comes near

   ________________ .

3. After Al and I punched in a code, the computer spoke to

   ________________ .

4. The cowboy prized his saddle and took good care of ________________ .
5. Ceres searched for her lovely daughter but couldn't find

   ________________ .

6. I gave the robot an order, and it followed ________________ around the room.

Possessive Pronouns

Possessive pronouns are used to show ownership or relationship.

Singular Possessive my, mine, your, yours, his, her, hers, its
Plural Possessive our, ours, your, yours, their, theirs

Possessive pronouns may be confused with contractions that are spelled similarly. Personal pronouns, however, never contain apostrophes. Look at the difference in these pairs.

Possessive Pronoun	The dog licked *its* paw.
Contraction	*It's* going to snow today. (It is)
Possessive Pronoun	*Their* costumes are in the wardrobe.
Contraction	*They're* moving to Nebraska. (They are)
Possessive Pronoun	*Your* film is being developed.
Contraction	*You're* next in line. (You are)

Using Possessive Pronouns and Contractions Underline the correct possessive pronoun or contraction in parentheses.

1. (Your, You're) probably afraid of alligators and crocodiles.
2. A fish's eyes are wide open even when (its, it's) asleep.
3. Monkeys take good care of (their, they're) young.
4. What are (your, you're) views on using animals in scientific experiments?
5. Because many birds eat insects, (their, they're) helpful to farmers.
6. The woodpecker uses (its, it's) sharp beak like a chisel.

Correcting Pronoun Errors Underline the error in a possessive pronoun or contraction. Then write the correct pronoun or contraction on the line.

1. You're ears are bombarded by all kinds of sounds. ____________
2. When your listening to the radio, do you turn up the volume? ____________
3. Some people lose they're hearing because of loud noises. ____________
4. Laws help protect people from loud noises while their at work. ____________
5. A boom from a jet can damage a building and break it's windows. ____________
6. Its important to learn about noise pollution. ____________

Indefinite Pronouns

An **indefinite pronoun** is a pronoun that does not refer to a specific person or a specific thing.

Singular Indefinite Pronouns

another	anything	everybody	neither	one
anybody	each	everyone	nobody	somebody
anyone	either	everything	no one	someone

Use the singular possessive pronouns *his, her,* and *its* with singular indefinite pronouns.

Plural Indefinite Pronouns

both many few several

Use the plural possessive pronoun *their* with plural indefinite pronouns.

Using Indefinite Pronouns Underline the possessive pronoun that agrees with the indefinite pronoun in each sentence.

1. Many of the early explorers risked (his or her, their) lives to discover new worlds.
2. Everybody can do (his or her, their) part in caring for the environment.
3. A few of the astronauts spent (his or her, their) time in the space station.
4. Neither of the knights lost (his, their) courage during the battle.
5. Everybody wrote a letter to the editor, expressing (his or her, their) opinion about the lyrics in rock songs.
6. Either of the contestants will have (his or her, their) chance to win a trip to Walt Disney World.
7. Both of the storytellers told (his or her, their) versions of how the world began.
8. Each of the scuba divers wore (his or her, their) face mask and snorkel.
9. One of the pitchers signed (his, their) autograph on my baseball.
10. Several of the sky divers jumped from the plane, opened (his or her, their) parachutes, and floated safely to the ground.

Linking Grammar and Writing: Understanding Pronouns

Write a paragraph introducing one of the following characters to some of your friends. The sentences of your paragraph should contain at least six pronouns: two as subjects, two as objects of verbs or prepositions, and two showing possession.

1. Count Dracula
2. Cinderella
3. a space creature
4. a superhero
5. a magician

Additional Practice: Understanding Pronouns

Pronouns and Antecedents Underline each pronoun in the following sentences. Draw an arrow to the antecedent of the pronoun.

1. Tornadoes can toss freight trains off their tracks.
2. The moon seems to be changing its shape constantly.
3. Medusa had hair made of snakes, and she could turn people into stone.
4. Dick Tracy wore a miniature two-way radio on his wrist.
5. The keys to the safe were missing, and the detective tried to find them.

Choosing the Correct Pronoun Underline the correct pronoun in each sentence.

1. Captain Hook was an evil pirate, and many feared his crew and (he, him).
2. The gull flapped (its, it's) wings and flew over the sea.
3. How often does (your, you're) heart beat?
4. A mother sea turtle lays her eggs and covers (they, them) with sand.
5. The winner of the poetry contest was (she, her).
6. A few of the warriors had painted (his, their) faces.
7. Bobby and (I, me) collect toys inspired by TV shows and movies.
8. Bats make very high–pitched sounds that (your, you're) unable to hear.
9. (Its, It's) difficult to predict when volcanoes will erupt.
10. Both of the pilots flew (his or her, their) planes in the air show.
11. Everybody cast (his or her, their) ballot for student-council president.
12. The feathers on birds keep (their, they're) bodies warm.
13. Each of the circus elephants stood on (its, their) hind legs.
14. (We, Us) adventurers explored Mammoth Cave in Kentucky.
15. The police noticed that someone had left (his or her, their) fingerprints on the doorknob.

Review: Understanding Pronouns

Finding Pronouns Underline each pronoun in the following sentences. Draw an arrow to the antecedent of the pronoun.

1. The tiger broke loose from its cage and roamed the city streets.
2. Annie Oakley joined the Buffalo Bill's Wild West show when she was twenty-five years old.
3. Tad is interested in stars and observes them through a telescope.
4. Gulliver traveled to a place called Lilliput, where he was a giant in a land of tiny people.

Substituting Pronouns for Nouns Rewrite the second sentence in each pair. Replace the repeated word or words with the correct subject pronoun, object pronoun, or possessive pronoun.

1. Do you know what a sari is? A sari is a long piece of cloth wrapped around the body like a dress.

   ____

2. Pecos Bill's early playmates were bears and wildcats. Pecos Bill's rope was as long as the equator.

   ____

3. Alice swims in a pool of her own tears. Alice also has other amazing adventures.

   ____

4. Rats were everywhere in the town of Hamelin. Fortunately, the Pied Piper led the rats away with his magical music.

   ____

Correcting Errors in Pronouns Underline each error in the use of pronouns. Then write the correction on the line.

1. Everyone should wear their safety belt. ______________
2. You're muscles are stretchy like rubber bands. ______________
3. Edgar and him claimed that they had seen a flying saucer. ______________
4. Several of the tourists brought they're cameras. ______________

What Are Adjectives?

An **adjective** is a word that modifies, or describes, a noun or pronoun. Two or more adjectives modifying the same word sometimes need to be separated with a comma.

dark, murky swamp   *black, furry* mask   *scary, powerful* giant

Some adjectives are made by adding endings to proper nouns. These are called **proper adjectives.** Always begin a proper adjective with a capital letter.

Australia + *-n* = Australian   Vietnam + *-ese* = Vietnamese

Other proper adjectives do not have special endings.

Hollywood movie   Idaho potato   Thanksgiving dinner

Finding Adjectives Draw one line under each common adjective and two lines under each proper adjective.

1. Colorful Navajo blankets are sold on Arizona reservations.
2. Most American colonists ate bread and cold meat for breakfast.
3. The powerful winds of a Kansas tornado blew off the roofs of many houses.
4. Long, sharp fangs and huge eyes were painted on the Chinese mask.
5. The Arabian desert contains the remains of ancient cities.
6. In Greek mythology the Minotaur was a horrible monster; it was half man, half wild bull.
7. In old Westerns, good cowboys wear white hats, and bad cowboys wear black hats.
8. Hawaiian leis are necklaces of beautiful flowers such as orchids.
9. Egyptian slaves helped build the gigantic pyramids.
10. On Halloween night, Orson Welles read a play about a Martian invasion.
11. The Alaskan pipeline took many years to complete.
12. Jack London described the terrible destruction of the San Francisco earthquake.
13. A diver found these Spanish coins along the Florida coast.
14. On maps, red lines may represent railroads, and blue lines may represent highways.

Kinds of Adjectives

Some adjectives tell *what kind:* *brave* crew, *dangerous* journey
Some adjectives tell *how many:* *ten* explorers, *many* adventures
Some adjectives tell *which ones:* *their* discoveries, *these* maps

Recognizing Adjectives Underline each adjective in the following sentences. Then label the adjective by writing *WK* for *what kind, HM* for *how many,* or *WO* for *which one.*

Example According to this (WO) old (WK) map, two (HM) roads lead to the magical (WK) city.

1. The popular cartoon *Peanuts* appears in over 2,000 newspapers in about 70 countries.
2. This snake has a poisonous bite.
3. In the early 1900s, young children had fewer toys than they do today.
4. His noisy old car needed a new muffler.
5. On the frontier, a teacher taught first grade through eighth grade in a schoolhouse with one room.
6. The empty building near our school used to be a busy factory.
7. The heavy rains caused mudslides throughout California.
8. The seven dwarfs lived in a tiny cottage in the middle of the forest.
9. A centipede may have 170 pairs of legs.
10. These mushrooms require dark, moist surroundings.

Using Adjectives Complete each sentence with the kind of adjective asked for in parentheses.

1. The ______________________ house at the edge of town looks haunted. (what kind)
2. ______________________ people in the town spotted a flying saucer. (how many)
3. Some of ______________________ dolls at the toy fair can walk and talk. (which ones)
4. The ______________________ dragon terrified all the people in the valley. (what kind)

Articles and Demonstrative Adjectives

The words *a, an,* and *the* are **articles**. Because these words always modify nouns, they are adjectives.

Use a before words beginning with consonant sounds.

a moth   a kilt   a rose   a horse   a cup

Use *an* before words beginning with vowel sounds.

an ant   an egg   an island   an ostrich   an uncle

A and *an* are used with singular nouns. *The* may be used before either a singular or a plural noun.

This, that, these, and *those* are **demonstrative adjectives.** They point out specific things. Use *this* and *that* with singular nouns: *this* boy, *that* kind of food. Use *these* and *those* with plural nouns: *these* boys, *those* kinds of vegetables.

This, that, these, or *those* is an adjective if it answers the question *which one* about a noun. It is a pronoun if it takes the place of a noun.

This bug is a beetle. (*adjective*) *This* is a beetle. (*pronoun*)

Them is always an object pronoun. It can never be used as an adjective.

Incorrect *Them* plants are healthy.
Correct *These* plants are healthy because I water *them.*

Using Articles and Demonstrative Adjectives Underline the correct word in parentheses.

1. (This, These) kind of deadly spider lives in the jungles of South America.
2. (This, Those) oriental rug we're standing on is fifty years old.
3. In the 1500s, Leonardo da Vinci made a design for (a, an) helicopter.
4. Did Bigfoot make (them, those) giant footprints in the snow?
5. (These, That) bird in the distance is a blue jay.
6. The glass bulbs of (a, an) hourglass contain grains of sand.
7. (This, These) kinds of doors are designed for people in wheelchairs.
8. A figure with eight sides is (a, an) octagon.
9. Nate collects these (sort, sorts) of comic books.
10. (Them, These) old white dresses are bridal gowns from the 1920s.

Predicate Adjectives

When an adjective follows a linking verb, it is part of the predicate. Therefore, it is called a **predicate adjective.** A predicate adjective modifies the subject.

The crocodiles *are* hungry.
The rock climbers *look* strong.

Here are some common linking verbs that often come before predicate adjectives:

am	was	become	look	taste
are	were	feel	seem	sound
is	appear	grow	smell	remain

Finding Predicate Adjectives Draw one line under the predicate adjective and two lines under the word it modifies in each of the following sentences.

1. Swimmers should be careful of dangerous sharks.
2. Puppies are helpless at birth.
3. The space creature in *E.T.: The Extraterrestrial* seems so friendly.
4. The surface of Mars appears reddish.
5. The Apaches were famous for their bravery and fierceness.
6. From the observation deck of the skyscraper, cars on the street look tiny.
7. Alice became very small after she drank the potion.
8. The spoiled milk tasted sour.
9. Dorothy felt sorry for the scarecrow without a brain.
10. The tornado in *The Wizard of Oz* grew powerful.

Using Predicate Adjectives Complete each sentence with a predicate adjective. Then underline the word it modifies.

1. During the hurricane, the waves became ______________________.
2. The puppy at the animal shelter looked so ______________________.
3. The records played on the old phonograph

   sounded ______________________.
4. Saturday morning cartoons are ______________________.
5. The stranger in the dark glasses seemed ______________________.

Making Comparisons with Adjectives

Use the **comparative form** of an adjective to compare two things. Add *-er* to form the comparative of most short adjectives.

My dog is *smaller* than my cat.

Use the **superlative form** of an adjective to compare three or more things. Add *-est* to form the superlative of most short adjectives.

My dog is the *smallest* of all the dogs on our block.

When an adjective has more than two syllables, the word *more* is usually used before the adjective to make the comparative form. Use the word *most* before the adjective to make the superlative form.

Adjective	Comparative Form	Superlative Form
difficult	more difficult	most difficult

Do not use *more* or *most* along with the *-er* or *-est* ending.

Incorrect The Sears Tower is more taller than the Hancock Building.
Correct The Sears Tower is taller than the Hancock Building.

Some adjectives use completely different words for the comparative and superlative forms.

Adjective	Comparative Form	Superlative Form
good	better	best
bad	worse	worst

Making Comparisons with Adjectives Underline the correct form of the adjective.

1. Superman is (faster, more fast) than a speeding bullet and (more powerful, most powerful) than a locomotive.
2. Tyrannosaurus was the (fiercest, most fierce) of all the dinosaurs.
3. Crocodiles are (smaller, more small), (thinner, more thin), and (quicker, more quicker) than alligators.
4. Jesse James was one of the (more famous, most famous) outlaws in the Wild West.
5. Are the California redwoods the (older, oldest) living trees in the world?
6. Air pollution is (worse, worser) in large cities than in the suburbs.
7. Pluto is the (smallest, most smallest) planet and is usually the (farthest, most far) from the sun.
8. African elephants are (larger, more larger) than Indian elephants and have (longer, longest) trunks.

Linking Grammar and Writing: Understanding Adjectives

1. You have an opportunity to rewrite a section of the well-known classic *The Wizard of Oz.* Dorothy will not visit Emerald City. She will visit whatever imaginary place *you* create.

Write a paragraph describing your imaginary place. Use many colorful and specific adjectives to describe the setting and to help your reader picture your special place. Remember that your readers will have no previous knowledge of the place you create. Use demonstrative adjectives to point out things that are near and things that are far.

2. Write at least five clues to help your friends guess a food you enjoy. Use predicate adjectives and comparative adjectives. For example, if your food is spaghetti, your first clue might be "It is *long* and *stringy.*" Your second clue might be "It is *tasteless* without sauce." A third clue might be "It is *softer* when it has been cooked than when it is uncooked." Exchange papers with your classmates and see who can guess the foods.

Additional Practice: Understanding Adjectives

Identifying Adjectives Underline the adjectives that modify each italicized noun in the sentences below. Include articles.

1. Diana, a Roman *goddess,* used moonbeams as arrows.
2. The *dungeon* of the castle was cold and damp.
3. Nine *planets* orbit the sun.
4. Alice has the most incredible *adventures* in Wonderland.
5. In the 1800s, Native Americans defended their sacred *lands.*
6. The fisherman's wife kept wishing for a bigger *home.*
7. Giraffes roam the hot African *plains.*
8. The cowboy wore a bright red *bandanna* to protect his face from the dust.
9. Those colorful *quilts* in the history museum are over a hundred years old.
10. Many *soldiers* in the Civil War were very young.

Using Adjectives Correctly Underline the correct word or words in parentheses.

1. Tall tales describe the (more incredible, most incredible) events.
2. These (kind, kinds) of stories are often about superheroes.
3. Paul Bunyan was one of the (greater, greatest) frontier heroes.
4. Paul Bunyan had (a, an) huge appetite.
5. He ate (more, most) food than other humans.
6. His stove covered (a, an) acre of land.
7. People today still enjoy (them, these) legends.
8. Many of the (funniest, most funny) tall tales are about the weather.
9. On one of the (hotter, hottest) days of the year, a river started boiling.
10. Carl Sandburg included some of the (better, best) tall tales in a poem.

Finding Adjectives Draw one line under each adjective and two lines under the word it modifies. Ignore articles.

1. During the spring, the days grow longer.
2. American colonists fought for independence during the Revolutionary War.
3. A sudden noise can cause a herd of elephants to stampede.
4. William Shakespeare compared the moon to a silvery bow.
5. Chicago is known as "The Windy City."
6. Robin Hood and his merry band of men lived in Sherwood Forest.
7. A shark has several rows of teeth.
8. The Irish flag is green, white, and gold.
9. Rip Van Winkle slept for twenty years.
10. The planet Saturn was named after the Roman god of agriculture.

Correcting Errors with Adjectives Underline the errors in the use of adjectives. Then correct the errors.

1. The moon is the most brightest object in the sky at night. ____________________
2. During the blizzard, the airport closed for a hour. ____________________
3. Health problems were worser a hundred years ago. ____________________
4. Were Laurel and Hardy the most funny comedy team in the 1930s? ____________________
5. Them trained seals over there play a tune on the horns. ____________________
6. Dorothy is powerfuller than the wicked witch. ____________________
7. Boris Karloff starred in an horror movie about a werewolf. ____________________
8. Which is strongest, hurricane winds or tornado winds? ____________________
9. Native Americans made these kind of canoes from tree barks. ____________________
10. Is Jupiter the larger planet in the solar system? ____________________

What Are Adverbs?

Adverbs modify verbs, adjectives, and other adverbs.

Liz ran *swiftly.* (*Swiftly* tells *how* Liz ran.)
The Washington County Dog Show begins *tomorrow.* (*Tomorrow* tells *when* the show begins.)
Three carpenters are working upstairs. (*Upstairs* tells *where* the carpenters are working.)
My sand sculpture is *nearly* finished. (*Nearly* tells *to what extent* the sand sculpture is finished.)

Many adverbs are formed by adding *-ly* to adjectives: quick + *-ly* = quickly. Other common adverbs include such words as *there, now, never, almost,* and *too.*

Finding Adverbs Draw one line under the adverb and two lines under the word it modifies in each of the following sentences.

Example The cymbals banged loudly.

1. Some early settlers nearly died from hunger and cold.
2. The octopus silently wrapped its tentacles around its prey.
3. The *Challenger* suddenly exploded in midair.
4. Charles Goodyear accidentally dropped rubber onto a hot stove.
5. Wonder Woman often used her magic lasso to capture villains.
6. Some homeless people sleep outside on park benches.
7. Imagine flying away to a distant planet!
8. Lincoln's most famous speech, the Gettysburg Address, lasted almost two minutes.
9. Now people are taking steps to preserve the earth's resources.
10. Sacagawea was a very brave member of the Lewis and Clark expedition.

Understanding Adverbs Underline the adverb in each sentence. Then show what the adverb tells by writing *How, When, Where,* or *To what extent.*

Example Gravity pulls the sky divers downward. Where

1. Pygmalion fell madly in love with a statue he created. ____________
2. Jane Addams was a very devoted social worker. ____________
3. The gold miners headed north to Alaska. ____________
4. Mozart's interest in music began early. ____________

Making Comparisons with Adverbs

Like adjectives, adverbs can be changed to comparative forms and superlative forms. Use the **comparative form** when you compare one action to another. Use the **superlative form** when you compare three or more actions.

Comparative Robin hit the ball *higher* than Marty.
Superlative Ruth hit the ball the *highest* of the three students.

The comparative and superlative forms of adverbs are formed in three ways.

1. **Some short adverbs add *-er* to form the comparative and *-est* to form the superlative.**

   fast faster fastest late later latest

2. **Most adverbs that end in *-ly* form the comparative with the word *more.* Form the superlative with the word *most.***

   quickly more quickly most quickly easily more easily most easily

3. **Some adverbs change completely to form the comparative and superlative.**

well	better	best	little	less	least
much	more	most	badly	worse	worst

Making Comparisons with Adverbs In each sentence underline the adverb that is used to make a comparison. Then identify the form of the adverb by writing *C* for *comparative* or *S* for *superlative.*

1. The wind blew harder as the storm approached. ____________
2. Which kind of shark is the least dangerous? ____________
3. Kangaroos are most commonly found in Australia. ____________
4. Hurricanes occur more often in summer than in winter. ____________

Using Adverbs in Comparisons Underline the correct form of the adverb in parentheses.

1. Redwood trees grow (taller, more tall) than any other trees in the forest.
2. The rain fell (steadilier, more steadily) than predicted.
3. The Yankee pitcher throws (harder, more hard) than the Dodger pitcher.
4. You can carry that pack on your shoulders (easilier, more easily) than in your hands.

Adjective or Adverb?

Because some adjectives and adverbs look very much alike, it is sometimes hard to know which type of word to use. To decide whether to use an adjective or an adverb, ask yourself what word is being modified.

The horses ran (quick, quickly.)
(*Quickly* is an adverb. It modifies the verb *ran*.)
It was a (real, really) close race.
(*Really* is an adverb. It modifies the adjective *close*.)

Remember, **adjectives** tell *which one, what kind,* or *how many.* They modify nouns and pronouns.

Adverbs tell *how, when, where,* or *to what extent.* They modify verbs, adjectives, and other adverbs.

Adjective or Adverb? Underline the correct modifier in parentheses.

1. The lion turned (sudden, suddenly) and growled.
2. The owl screeched (shrill, shrilly) and snatched its prey.
3. Houdini's magic act was (real, really) amazing.
4. In the 1800s, some women felt (angry, angrily) because they were denied the right to vote.
5. The cattle were (terrible, terribly) nervous before the storm.
6. Robots can be programmed to paint cars (careful, carefully).
7. Robin Hood's friend Little John was (actual, actually) over seven feet tall.
8. Batman looked (suspicious, suspiciously) at Cat Woman.
9. Butch Cassidy became (famous, famously) for his train robberies.
10. John Muir was (sure, surely) a pioneer in protecting wildlife.

Using Adjectives and Adverbs Correctly Underline each error in the use of modifiers. Then write the correct modifier.

1. The pirate Captain Hook was real afraid of the crocodile. ____________
2. Albert Einstein thought creative about the universe. ____________
3. Jackie Robinson was sure an outstanding baseball player. ____________
4. The rings around the planet Saturn look so colorfully. ____________
5. Ella Fitzgerald sang beautiful. ____________

Using Good *and* Well, *and* Bad *and* Badly

Good and *bad* are adjectives. They tell *what kind.*

Those peaches look *good.* (*Look* is used as a linking verb here. Therefore, *good* is a predicate adjective that modifies *peaches.*)

I feel *bad* about the homeless. (*Feel* is a linking verb. *Bad* is a predicate adjective.)

The words *well* and *badly* are adverbs. Use them to modify verbs. *Well* and *badly* tell *how* something is done.

Jon behaved *badly.* (*Badly* tells *how* Jon behaved.)

Ellen dances *well.* (*Well* tells *how* Ellen dances.)

Well is an adjective when it describes a noun or pronoun and means "healthy."

Brad does not feel *well.*

Using *Good* and *Well,* and *Bad* and *Badly* Underline the correct word in parentheses.

1. Cats can see (good, well) in the dark.
2. After the storm the pier was damaged (bad, badly).
3. The fumes from the factory smelled (bad, badly).
4. Lila took medicine that helped her feel (good, well) again.
5. UNICEF helps children who need food (bad, badly).
6. Denzel Washington performs his roles (good, well).
7. Many people feel (bad, badly) about the use of animals in experiments.
8. Everyone at the jazz festival had a (good, well) time.
9. Comic-book characters are often either (good, well) or evil.
10. The wolf in "Little Red Riding Hood" behaved (bad, badly).
11. In the 1830s, the Cherokees were treated very (bad, badly).
12. Sylvia looked (good, well) in her mermaid costume.

Double Negatives

Several words are used to say "not." These words are called **negatives**. *No, no one, not, none, nobody, nowhere, nothing,* and *never* are negatives. Contractions that end in *-n't* are also negatives: *can't, don't, doesn't, wouldn't, won't,* and *isn't.*

When two negatives appear in one sentence, they result in a **double negative**. Avoid double negatives when you write and speak.

Incorrect The stray puppy didn't have nowhere to sleep.
Correct The stray puppy didn't have anywhere to sleep.
Correct The stray puppy had nowhere to sleep.

Using Negatives Underline the correct word in parentheses.

1. Many pioneers searched for gold but didn't find (any, none).
2. Nobody had seen (any, no) spaceship land in the desert.
3. Gerry couldn't believe that astronauts would (ever, never) go to Mars.
4. No one could do (anything, nothing) to control the robot's actions.
5. Elena hadn't (ever, never) heard the story about the headless horseman.

Correcting Double Negatives Rewrite the sentences to eliminate the double negatives. Some sentences can be corrected in more than one way.

1. A shepherd boy cried "Wolf!" three times even though there wasn't no wolf. ______________________________

____

2. Neighbors couldn't find a wolf nowhere.

____

3. Later, they didn't pay no attention to the shepherd boy's cries for help.

____

____

4. Since the wolf didn't have nothing to fear, he started attacking the sheep.

____

____

5. No one never believes a liar, even when he or she is telling the truth.

____

Linking Grammar and Writing: Understanding Adverbs

Imagine that you have just invented a new piece of sports equipment for a game or activity you enjoy. It might be an ultrasonic bat that never misses a pitched ball, or perhaps a pair of jogging shoes designed to prevent fatigue.

Write a description of your special new equipment, telling exactly what it does. Use many descriptive adverbs to tell how, when, and where your equipment excels. Use comparative adjectives and adverbs to relate your equipment to similar products already available at stores.

Additional Practice: Understanding Adverbs

Identifying Adverbs Underline the adverb in each sentence. Then show what the adverb tells by writing *How, When, Where,* or *To what extent.*

1. The tail of a comet points away from the sun. ____________________
2. Mirrors were first used in Europe during the 1500s. ____________________
3. The electric guitar screeched loudly. ____________________
4. The White Rabbit was very late for his appointment. ____________________
5. The horse in the rodeo kicked its legs wildly. ____________________

Choosing the Right Word Underline the correct word in parentheses.

1. The search party couldn't find the bandits (anywhere, nowhere).
2. Which costs (less, least), a mountain bike or a racing bike?
3. Playing video games helps many students learn to use a computer (good, well).
4. In marathon dances, the couple who danced (longer, longest) won a prize.
5. Rapunzel couldn't find (any, no) escape from the tower.
6. Who led his troops (better, best) during the Civil War— General Grant or General Lee?
7. In the 1940s, Preston Tucker tried to design the (more safely, most safely) built car on the road.
8. Some Doberman pinschers look (mean, meanly).
9. There wasn't (anybody, nobody) who could solve the mystery.
10. Alex called the doctor because he didn't feel (good, well).
11. The sea captain could hardly see (anything, nothing) in the thick fog.
12. American colonists felt that England's laws were (real, really) unfair.
13. Maurice Sendak's pictures in *Where the Wild Things Are* look so (strange, strangely).
14. In the 1950s, girls weren't allowed to play on (any, no) Little League teams.
15. Amelia Earhart was (sure, surely) a pioneer in the history of flight.

Review: Understanding Adverbs

Finding Adverbs Draw one line under the adverb and two lines under the word or words it modifies in each of the following sentences.

1. The dodo bird has vanished forever.
2. The magician waved his magic wand, and suddenly a white dove appeared.
3. The Mad Hatter is a rather unusual character.
4. People once believed that the world was flat.
5. Almost every person in the United States owns a television set.

Using Modifiers Correctly Underline each error in the use of an adjective or adverb. Then write the correct modifier.

1. A stunt person's job can be real dangerous. ____________________
2. Oliver Twist looked badly in his tattered old clothes. ____________________
3. Kristi Yamaguchi skated beautiful in the Olympics. ____________________
4. The recording of John F. Kennedy's speeches sounded incredibly. ____________________
5. The turtle waddled slow across the road. ____________________

Choosing the Correct Adverb Underline the correct word in parentheses.

1. Who ran (faster, fastest), the tortoise or the hare?
2. Stephen King's stories are often (real, really) scary.
3. Beethoven couldn't hear (any, no) notes of his own music because he was deaf.
4. The fox jumped (higher, more higher) but still couldn't reach the grapes.
5. The Amish and the Quakers don't believe in fighting in (any, no) wars.
6. Do elephants live (longer, longest) of all animals?
7. Rachel Carson felt (bad, badly) about the effects of DDT, a powerful insect killer, on the environment.
8. The waves crashed (violent, violently) against the rocky shore.
9. The frog prince couldn't do (anything, nothing) to break the magic spell.
10. In the 1800s, children who worked in factories were treated (bad, badly).

Skills Assessment 2

Directions One or more of the underlined sections in the following sentences may contain an error in grammar, usage, punctuation, spelling, or capitalization. Write the letter of each incorrect section. Then rewrite the section correctly. If there is no error in an item, write D.

Example Pioneers led really (A) hard lives, some (B) early settlers near (C) perished from cold and hunger. No error (D)

Answer **B**—lives. Some;
C—nearly

1. The first Olympic Games were held (A) in ancient Greece. Each of the athletes tried their (B) best to please the Greek gods and to honor dead heros. (C) No error (D)

2. Our (A) amusement park will open it's (B) doors this weekend with two new roller coasters. I wonder which is the fastest. (C) No error (D)

3. About 35,000 years ago, Cro-Magnon people used (A) sewing needles made of bone. These kind (B) of tools are among humans' earlyest (C) inventions. No error (D)

4. There weren't no (A) big toy factories (B) in the 1800s. During that time, childrens' (C) toys were homemade. No error (D)

5. Crazy Horse was an Oglala Sioux chief. He (A) fought (B) General Custer in 1876 at the Battle of Little Bighorn. Many people remember both Custer and he (C) because of that battle. No error (D)

6. The Everglades is a real (A) interesting place to visit. Its (B) a big, swampy area in south Florida. (C) No error (D)

7. The world's biggest (A) reflecting telescope is located on a (B) hawaiin (C) mountaintop. No error (D)

8. Daryl hits the baseball more farther with a lighter bat. He couldn't
A B
swing as quick with a heavier bat. No error
C D

9. We saw some monarch butterflies in you're garden. Both Marta and I
A B
tried to photograph them. No error
C D

10. Is there too much violence on television? Some of us wrote letters to
A B
the major networks and expressed our opinions. No error
C D

11. Our band didn't play too bad in rehearsal. I feel confidently that tonight
A B
we will also perform well. No error
C D

12. Superman could make a diamond. By crushing a lump of coal in his
A B
hands. How powerful and strong was he! No error
C D

13. The Boy Scouts and their families had a potluck meal, and everybody

brought his or her own dish. Lee couldn't decide which he liked best,
A B C
chili or stuffed pizza. No error
D

14. Some scientists believe the world is getting warmer. Planting more
A B C
trees may help prevent rising temperatures. No error
D

15. Some towns in the united states bury their trash. Them dumps are
A B C
called landfills. No error
D

What Are Prepositions?

A **preposition** shows how a noun or a pronoun relates to another word in the sentence.

> Warren leaned *against* the wall.
> *Into* the pond slid the lizard.
> The pitcher threw the ball *to* me.

In these sentences, the words *against, into,* and *to* are prepositions. The noun or pronoun following a preposition is called the **object of the preposition**. The words *wall, pond,* and *me* are objects of prepositions in the sentences above. Here is a list of commonly used prepositions:

about	before	down	of	to
above	behind	during	off	toward
across	below	for	on	under
after	beneath	from	onto	underneath
against	beside	in	out	until
along	between	inside	outside	up
among	beyond	into	over	upon
around	but (except)	like	past	with
at	by	near	through	without

Finding Prepositions In each sentence below, underline each preposition once and the object of that preposition twice.

1. A tugboat pushes barges down the river.
2. The pinch hitter drove the ball deep into left field.
3. The Sioux people depended greatly on the buffalo.
4. The air force jets disappeared behind the clouds.
5. Dr. Frankenstein conducted amazing experiments in his laboratory.

Using Prepositions Complete each of the sentences with a preposition.

1. George W. G. Ferris built a huge wheel that carried passengers _______________ its outside rim.
2. Native Americans make moccasins _______________ dried animal skins.
3. The word *pajamas* comes _______________ the Persian language.
4. Treasure hunters found gold _______________ the coast of Florida.
5. The detective examined the fingerprints _______________ his magnifying glass.

Using Prepositional Phrases

A **prepositional phrase** is a group of words that begins with a preposition and ends with its object. The preposition, its object, and all the words that describe the object form a prepositional phrase.

My cousin hid *behind the first door.* (*Door* is the object of the preposition *behind.)*
The coach was looking *for Susan.* (*Susan* is the object of the preposition *for.*)

A prepositional phrase may have a **compound object** made up of two or more nouns joined by *and* or *or.*

We used bricks made *of red clay and straw.*

You can often make your writing smoother by reducing a sentence to a prepositional phrase and combining it with another sentence.

We tossed coins. We tossed them *into a fountain.*
We tossed coins *into a fountain.*

Finding Prepositional Phrases Underline each prepositional phrase in the sentences below. There may be more than one prepositional phrase in a sentence.

1. Make a walkie-talkie with two empty cans.
2. Punch a hole through the bottom of each can.
3. Find a piece of sturdy string about twenty feet long.
4. Push one end of the string through the hole in one of the cans.
5. Tie a large knot at the end of the string.
6. Repeat the preceding two steps with the other can.

Using Prepositional Phrases Rewrite each of the following pairs of sentences by reducing one sentence to a prepositional phrase and combining it with the other sentence.

1. The cowboys rode their horses. They rode into the sunset.

____

2. Read the poem "Mother to Son." It is by Langston Hughes.

____

3. James Thurber wrote a funny fable. It is about a bird and two chipmunks.

____

4. Suddenly, the clock stopped. It stopped at midnight.

____

Pronouns After Prepositions

Use the object forms of pronouns as objects of prepositions. The object forms are *me, you, him, her, it, us,* and *them.*

Mary Kay took an umbrella with *her.*
Three swans were gliding toward *them.*

Sometimes a pronoun is part of a **compound object of a preposition.** When a pronoun is used as part of a compound object, use an object pronoun.

Simple Object	**Compound Object**
We sat with *Gary.*	We sat with *Gary* and *her.*
Toss the ball to *Martha.*	Toss the ball to *Martha* and *me.*

If you are confused about which pronoun form to use, say the sentence with just the pronoun following the preposition. Then write the sentence with the complete prepositional phrase.

Dana gave the tickets to Sarah and (he, him).
Dana gave the tickets to *him.*
Dana gave the tickets to Sarah and him.

Using Pronouns After Prepositions In each sentence, underline the preposition once and the pronoun used as its object twice.

1. The museum's dinosaur expert was talking to us.
2. We toured the museum with her.
3. Behind her was a giant skeleton labeled "Tyrannosaurus."
4. We walked around it and gaped.
5. The teeth were six inches long—there were rows of them!
6. Near me was a fascinating display: "Stegosaurus Eggs."
7. Above us hung a pterodactyl, a huge flying reptile.
8. "How many of you have questions?" the expert asked.
9. "What happened to them?" I asked.
10. The expert explained that no one knows exactly what happened to them.

Using the Correct Pronoun as Object Underline the correct pronoun in parentheses.

1. We sent a birthday card to (he, him) and (she, her).
2. The reward money was divided between Carlos and (I, me).
3. The crowd gathered around the witnesses and (they, them).
4. Aunt Ella and I played dominoes against Shelly and (she, her).
5. The police officer asked for an explanation from (they, them) or (we, us).

More About Prepositions

Several words that are used as prepositions are also used as adverbs. If the word begins a phrase, it is probably a preposition. If it is used alone, it is probably an adverb.

The old steam engine chugged *past.* (adverb)
The old steam engine chugged *past* the station. (preposition)

The prepositions *between* and *among* often cause confusion. Use *between* to refer to two persons, objects, or groups. Use *among* to refer to three or more persons, objects, or groups.

Choose *between* the apple and the pear.
The popcorn will be divided *among* Russ, Orlando, and me.

Identifying Prepositions and Adverbs Label each italicized word *Adverb* or *Preposition.*

1. The batter walked *to* the plate. ____________________
2. He planted his feet and looked *up.* ____________________
3. The pitcher stood *on* the mound. ____________________
4. The pitcher looked *around,* wound up, and threw the ball. ____________________
5. The batter swung *at* the ball and missed. ____________________
6. Then the batter hit a grounder and ran *toward* first base. ____________________
7. The umpire jerked his thumb *over* his shoulder. ____________________
8. The base runner jumped *up* and began to argue. ____________________

Using Prepositions Correctly Underline the correct word in parentheses.

1. Pony Express riders carried mail (between, among) St. Joseph, Missouri, and Sacramento, California.
2. (Between, Among) all the characters in the *Peanuts* cartoon, Charlie Brown is my favorite.
3. After Beethoven became deaf, he played the piano with a long stick (between, among) his teeth.
4. Health problems are common (between, among) coal miners.

What Are Conjunctions?

A **conjunction** joins words or groups of words. The conjunctions *and, but,* and *or* can join compound sentence parts.

Jack *and* Virginia will collect the papers. (*And* joins subjects.)
Carol caught the ball *but* then dropped it. (*But* joins predicates.)
Was the note for you *or* me? (*Or* joins objects of a preposition.)

The conjunctions *and, but,* and *or* can also join closely related sentences.

The theater lights dimmed. The curtain went up.
The theater lights dimmed, *and* the curtain went up.

A comma is used at the end of the first sentence, before the conjunction.

Identifying Compound Constructions Underline the compound part in each of the following sentences and label it *Subject, Predicate, Object,* or *Sentence.*

1. Thunder rumbled in the distance, but the sun was shining here. ____________
2. All animals need food, water, and shelter. ____________
3. In some places, oxen or horses are still used to pull plows. ____________
4. Thoreau moved to Walden Pond and built a home there. ____________

Sentence Combining Combine each of the following pairs of sentences into a single sentence. Choose a conjunction and use a comma if necessary. Omit words in italics.

1. On the merry-go-round you can ride a horse. *You can ride* a lion.

____

2. The Confederate troops won many battles. The Union troops won the Civil War. ____

____

3. At the history museum, a log cabin was on display. An old locomotive *was on display.* ____

____

4. The paper airplane climbed steeply. *The paper airplane* then dived into the ground. ____

____

Using Words as Different Parts of Speech

Some words can be used as several different parts of speech.

The *ticket* sales are slow. (*Ticket* is an adjective.)
I have a *ticket* for the concert. (*Ticket* is a noun.)
The officers *ticketed* the driver. (*Ticketed* is a verb.)

To decide what part of speech a word is, you must see how it is used in a sentence.

Identifying Parts of Speech Tell what part of speech the word in italics is in each sentence. On the blank, write *Noun, Verb, Adjective, Adverb,* or *Preposition.*

1. Larry should *iron* his shirt. ____________ *Iron* is mined in Minnesota. ____________
2. The *line* graph showed changes in costs. ____________ We will *line* the shelves with paper. ____________
3. John Wayne *starred* in many movies. ____________ Sailors navigate by the North *Star.* ____________
4. *Hand* me the tickets, please. ____________ Randy cut his *hand.* ____________
5. The carpenter made *kitchen* cabinets. ____________ The *kitchen* of the farmhouse was huge. ____________
6. The batter hit an *outside* pitch. ____________ The ball went *outside* the yard. ____________
7. The mayor gave a *talk* to our class. ____________ *Talk* to Elaine about your idea. ____________
8. The clock *strikes* at three. ____________ Mandy bowled two *strikes* in a row. ____________
9. I don't feel *well.* ____________ We get our water from a *well.* ____________
10. Lynn finished the race in *record* time. ____________ Ron collects *records* from the 1960s. ____________

Linking Grammar and Writing: Understanding Prepositions and Conjunctions

Imagine that you are a tour guide in your city. The regular bus driver is ill, and your new driver doesn't know the route. Before the tour begins, give the new bus driver directions for a tour that will stop at three major attractions in your hometown. The tour will begin in front of the Four Star Hotel and end at your last attraction. Write your directions in paragraph form. Underline each preposition and circle each conjunction that you use.

Additional Practice: Understanding Prepositions and Conjunctions

Finding Prepositions and Objects In the following sentences, draw one line under each preposition and two lines under the object of that preposition.

1. The newspapers near the checkout line in the supermarket contain articles about incredible events.
2. Here are some examples of unusual headlines.
3. Couple from Wyoming spots Elvis Presley at a ranch.
4. Twelve-year-old boy sees a ghost walk through a wall.

Using Pronouns and Prepositions Underline the correct pronoun or preposition in parentheses.

1. Spain is located (between, among) France and Portugal.
2. The woman showed Lester and (I, me) how to make candles.
3. (Between, Among) all of his Muppet creations, Jim Henson liked Kermit the Frog the best.
4. The fortuneteller made predictions about (he, him) and (she, her).

Using Conjunctions Write each sentence pair as a single sentence, using *and, but,* or *or.* Add commas where needed. Omit italicized words.

1. Coins were usually gold. *They were also* silver.

   ____

2. The hot-air balloon rose up. *It* drifted over the streets of Paris.

   ____

3. Sky diving looks fun. *It* can be a dangerous sport.

   ____

4. Laser beams weld car parts. *Laser beams* check the cars' fuel systems.

   ____

Identifying Parts of Speech Identify the part of speech of each italicized word.

1. The top spun *around* wildly. ____________
2. Phileas Fogg traveled *around* the world in eighty days. ____________
3. *Telephone* the weather bureau if you spot a tornado. ____________
4. Thirteen blackbirds were perched on the *telephone* line. ____________

Review: Understanding Prepositions and Conjunctions

Using Prepositions In each sentence, draw one line under each preposition and two lines under the object of that preposition.

1. Launch your paper airplane in your back yard.
2. Put one or two paper clips on the plane.
3. Hold the body of the airplane between your thumb and finger.
4. Throw the airplane into the wind.

Using Pronouns and Prepositions Correctly Underline the correct word in parentheses.

1. The members of the jury discussed the verdict (between, among) themselves.
2. The butler showed the secret passageway to the detective and (we, us).
3. The Golden Gate Bridge is a link (between, among) San Francisco and Marin County.
4. The lion in the cage growled at you and (I, me).

Identifying Compound Constructions Underline the compound part in each of the following sentences and label it *Subject, Predicate, Object,* or *Sentence.*

1. The judge banged his gavel and brought the court to order. ____________
2. The clown dressed like a tramp and had a very sad face. ____________
3. Was the lady or the tiger behind the door? ____________
4. The knight tried to pull the sword from the stone, but he failed. ____________

Identifying Parts of Speech Identify the part of speech of each italicized word.

1. Fans waited *outside* the stage door for the rock star. ____________
2. During the summer the actors perform plays *outside.* ____________
3. The folk dancer *stamps* her feet and taps a tambourine. ____________
4. Rare *stamps* were on display at the post office. ____________

Subject and Verb Agreement

A verb must **agree in number** with its subject. A subject and a verb agree in number when they are both singular or both plural.

Singular verbs in the present tense usually end in *s* or *es.* They are used with singular subjects. Plural verbs in the present tense do not usually end in *s* or *es.* When the subject is plural, the verb must be plural too.

Singular	**Plural**
One *cloud floats* in the sky.	Many *clouds float* in the sky.
A *snake hisses.*	*Snakes hiss.*

Making Subjects and Verbs Agree Underline the verb that agrees with the subject.

1. Two contestants on the game show (ties, tie) for first place.
2. Many people (exercises, exercise) by lifting weights.
3. Each year, many tourists (visits, visit) the White House.
4. The children (explores, explore) an old attic at a museum in Boston.
5. The sports announcer (gives, give) a play-by-play account of the game.
6. The Dewey Decimal System (classifies, classify) books in the library.
7. The bike trail (stretches, stretch) three miles across town.
8. Two seals (dives, dive) into the icy water to catch fish.
9. Smoke (curls, curl) from the chimney.
10. Most mysteries (ends, end) with the arrest of the guilty suspect.
11. Some people in New Guinea (eats, eat) insects for protein.
12. The roadside diner (serves, serve) country breakfasts.
13. House cats (likes, like) to stalk birds.
14. The butterflies (swarms, swarm) over the pine trees.
15. Bugs Bunny (chews, chew) on a carrot and says, "What's up, Doc?"

Agreement with Special Verbs

Some verbs have special forms. Follow the rules of agreement for these verbs.

Is, Was, Are, Were The verb forms *is* and *was* are singular. The forms *are* and *were* are plural.

Singular	Naomi *is* at the door.	Naomi *was* at the door.
Plural	The boys *are* in the boat.	The boys *were* in the boat.

Has, Have The verb form *has* is singular. The form *have* is plural.

Singular Gene *has washed* the car.
Plural They *have washed* the car.

Does, Do The verb form *does* is singular. The form *do* is plural.

Singular Sandy *does* the raking.
Plural They *do* the raking.

There is, Where is, Here is In a sentence that begins with *there, where,* or *here,* the subject usually comes after the verb. Find the subject first and decide whether it is singular or plural. Then choose the right verb form to agree with the subject.

There *are* (V) several *bands* (S) in the parade. (The subject and the verb are plural.)

Where *is* (V) your *trombone* (S)? (The subject and the verb are singular.)

Using the Correct Verb Form Underline the correct form of the verb.

1. Some people really (does, do) believe in flying saucers.
2. There (is, are) crabs scuttling along the shore.
3. Two ski poles (was, were) standing in the drift.
4. The toy store (has, have) a giant video screen.
5. Where (does, do) geese fly each fall?
6. (Is, Are) there a weather station near you?
7. Native American war bonnets (was, were) made with long feathers.
8. No two people (has, have) the same fingerprints.
9. The witness said, "Here (is, are) a description of the thieves."
10. (Does, Do) the magician amaze you?

Special Agreement Problems

Compound Subjects When two or more parts of a compound subject are joined by *and,* use a plural verb.

> *Carol* and *Becky are* my best friends.
> The *bike* and the *skateboard were* expensive.

When the parts of the subject are joined by *or, either/or,* or *neither/nor,* use the form of the verb that agrees with the part closest to the verb.

> Mark or *Ramon is making* the list.
> Neither Susan nor her *sisters know* the new student.

Prepositional Phrases After the Subject Do not confuse the subject of a verb with the object of a preposition.

> The *gate* near the pines *makes* squeaky noises.
> *Gate* is the subject of the sentence.
> *Gate* is singular, so you use the singular verb *makes.*
> *Near the pines* is a prepositional phrase. The verb agrees with the subject, not with the object of the preposition.

Choosing the Right Verb In each sentence, underline the verb that agrees with the subject.

1. The sound of beating drums (fills, fill) the room.
2. A sea horse's head and neck (resembles, resemble) a real horse's.
3. Many people in the desert (uses, use) jeeps instead of camels.
4. Neither a racehorse nor an antelope (runs, run) faster than a cheetah.
5. The giant statues on Easter Island (is, are) a mystery.
6. During a drought, rivers and lakes (dries, dry) up.
7. The lute and the mandolin (was, were) popular Renaissance musical instruments.
8. The roots of a plant (stores, store) food.
9. The wings of a hummingbird (moves, move) very quickly.
10. Most members of the cat family (is, are) clever hunters.
11. Either a squirrel or a raccoon (lives, live) in this hollow log.
12. An empty jug or an old boot (is, are) sometimes the home of a house wren.
13. A rabbit's foot or a four-leaf clover (is, are) a good-luck charm.
14. In the 1800s, the horse stable and the railroad station (was, were) important places in a town.
15. The scenic trail through the mountains (is, are) eight miles long.

Agreement with Pronouns

I and You Although *I* stands for a single person, the only singular verb forms used with *I* are *am* and *was.* Otherwise, the plural form of the verb is always used.

I *am* tired.	I *am going* home now.	I *was* hungry.
I *have* two sisters.	I *write* poetry.	I *speak* Spanish.

Although *you* can be singular or plural, always use a plural verb with this pronoun.

"You *were* late," the coach said to the player.
"You *were* late," the coach said to the players.

Indefinite Pronouns The pronouns below are singular and must be used with singular verbs.

each	either	everyone	anyone	no one
one	neither	everybody	anybody	nobody

Do not be confused when a prepositional phrase follows one of these pronouns. The verb must still agree with the pronoun subject.

Neither of these watches *works.*

Choosing the Right Verb In each sentence, underline the verb that agrees with the subject.

1. Have you heard the "I (Has, Have) a Dream" speech of Martin Luther King, Jr.?
2. Nobody (knows, know) exactly how long it took to build the Great Pyramid.
3. You (makes, make) a Halloween mask from a paper bag.
4. Before the game starts, everyone at the ballpark (sings, sing) "The Star-Spangled Banner."
5. Neither of the witnesses (was, were) telling the truth.
6. Almost everybody (wonders, wonder) what life will be like in the twenty-first century.
7. Every one of the astronauts (undergoes, undergo) many months of training.
8. You (sees, see) Arabian, Chinese, and Spanish dances in *The Nutcracker.*
9. Either of the mummies (is, are) thousands of years old.
10. Someone in the haunted house suddenly (hears, hear) a scream.

Linking Grammar and Writing: Mastering Subject-Verb Agreement

Imagine that you are an entertainment reporter broadcasting live from this year's pop music awards presentation.

Using lively verbs in the present tense, write a description of the performers as they step up to the stage to receive their awards. Include details that will add interest to your writing.

Pay particular attention to subject-verb agreement. Be sure that you use the singular form of a verb when your subject is singular. Use the plural form of a verb when your subject is plural. Be careful when a prepositional phrase comes after the subject. Do not confuse the subject of the verb with the object of the preposition.

Additional Practice: Mastering Subject-Verb Agreement

Choosing Correct Verb Forms Underline the correct verb in parentheses.

1. These castles (was, were) built during the Middle Ages.
2. Each of the soldiers (salutes, salute) the flag.
3. The Celts (was, were) the first group to invade England.
4. How (does, do) you sort trash for recycling?
5. Here (is, are) the meaning of the secret code.
6. The gymnast (does, do) a back flip on the balance beam.
7. Sleet and hail (is, are) frozen raindrops.
8. Where (was, were) the hideout of Butch Cassidy and the Sundance Kid?
9. A meteor (is, are) a rock from outer space.
10. Smoke and dust (pollutes, pollute) the air.
11. I (shapes, shape) the clay on a potter's wheel.
12. People in the factory (wears, wear) earplugs to protect their hearing.
13. The cat (pounces, pounce) on a toy mouse.
14. Somebody (speeds, speed) down a country road in the middle of the night.
15. Many communities (buries, bury) their trash in landfills.
16. Everyone in class (enjoys, enjoy) stories about space travel.
17. This kind of paint (glows, glow) in the dark.
18. The lights in the theater (dims, dim) as the curtain rises.
19. Neither of these magic tricks (is, are) easy to perform.
20. A stuntwoman in movies (takes, take) many risks.
21. Animals in a wildlife preserve (is, are) safe from hunters.
22. (Has, Have) you ever seen yourself in a fun-house mirror?
23. (Does, Do) tadpoles have legs?
24. Jupiter, Saturn, and Uranus (has, have) rings.
25. There (is, are) an incredible world underneath the sea.

Review: Mastering Subject-Verb Agreement

Choosing Correct Verb Forms Underline the verb that agrees with the subject in each sentence.

1. Neither the architect nor the engineers (knows, know) why the bridge fell.
2. You (holds, hold) chopsticks between your thumb and first finger.
3. Everyone in our class (has, have) seen the sky show at the planetarium.
4. Rita and Lester (reads, read) legends about King Arthur's brave deeds.
5. The counselor (leads, lead) the campers on a hike through the woods.
6. The African mask (was, were) decorated with beads and shells.
7. In the 1950s, there (was, were) many popular TV series about family life.
8. I (wishes, wish) that I could travel in a time machine.
9. The Lincoln Memorial in Washington, D.C., (is, are) made of marble.
10. Armor from the Middle Ages (is, are) on display at the art museum.
11. One of the oddest inventions (was, were) goggles for chickens.
12. The TV reporter said, "Here (is, are) today's top news stories."
13. In the movie *Harvey,* a man (talks, talk) to an imaginary rabbit.
14. I (watches, watch) a caterpillar spin its cocoon.
15. How (does, do) a scientist put together a dinosaur skeleton from a pile of bones?
16. A hamster or a turtle (makes, make) a good pet.
17. Each of the satellites (sends, send) weather information back to earth.
18. Some commercials on TV (persuades, persuade) children to buy products.
19. Ramps and wider doors (helps, help) people in wheelchairs enter and leave buildings.
20. Cirrus clouds (looks, look) like soft white feathers.
21. Almost everyone (celebrates, celebrate) the Fourth of July.
22. Where (does, do) the longest animal live?
23. The movements in an Asian dance often (tells, tell) a story.
24. Many divers (has, have) searched the ocean floor for treasure ships.
25. There (is, are) three main oceans in the world.

Skills Assessment 3

Directions One or more of the underlined sections in the following sentences may contain an error in grammar, usage, punctuation, spelling, or capitalization. Write the letter of each incorrect section. Then rewrite the section correctly. If there is no error in an item, write *D.*

Example The acrobats and the clowns form (A) a pyramid. Each give (B) strength and suport (C) to the figure. No error (D)

Answer B—gives
C—support

1. You often see (A) monarch butterflys (B) in the summer, (C) but in the fall they disappear. No error (D)

2. Tom, our friend from England, (A) made toad-in-the-hole for Rex and I. (B) It's (C) sausage cooked in a batter. No error (D)

3. Many kinds of mushrooms grow (A) in these woods. Between (B) them, only a few is (C) safe to eat. No error (D)

4. The movement of the clouds were (A) barely visible and (B) the water was (C) as smooth as glass. No error (D)

5. The crumbs (A) of moldy bread is (B) used to make Roquefort, a kind of french (C) cheese. No error (D)

6. Do you have (A) another computer disk. (B) This one on my desk is nearly (C) full. No error (D)

7. Typhoons and hurricanes occur (A) from midsummer to early Fall. (B) Typhoons form (C) in the western Pacific Ocean; hurricanes form in the Atlantic. No error (D)

8. There's (A) two (B) flightless birds native to Australia—the cassowary and (C) the emu. No error (D)

9. Where do (A) clowns learn about makeup and tricks? Is (B) there a school for them, or do they get their (C) training on the job? No error (D)

10. The geyser sprayed warm water all over the guide and us. (A) Everyone got his or her (B) clothes really (C) wet. No error (D)

11. Quito Ecuador, (A) lays (B) almost exactly on the equator. However, (C) the climate there is quite mild. No error (D)

12. The magician and his pretty assistant entertains (A) the audience with their (B) trick. Her body raises (C) and hangs above the table. No error (D)

13. The bells of those two churchs (A) have rang (B) every Christmas Eve (C) for almost a century. No error (D)

14. Many authors uses (A) pseudonyms. Neither Mark Twain nor Dr. Seuss (B) wrote under their (C) own name. No error (D)

15. The detective moved cautious (A) into the dark hallway. He felt (B) strange (C) in this lonely place. No error (D)

Proper Nouns and Proper Adjectives

A **common noun** is a general name of a person, place, thing, or idea. A **proper noun** names a particular person, place, thing, or idea. A **proper adjective** is made from a proper noun. All proper nouns and adjectives are capitalized.

Common Noun	Proper Noun	Proper Adjective
queen	**E**lizabeth	**E**lizabethan
country	**M**exico	**M**exican

A proper noun can be made up of one or more words. Capitalize all important words in a proper noun.

New **Y**ear's **D**ay **O**hio **R**iver **P**eter the **G**reat

Proper adjectives are often used with common nouns. Do not capitalize the common noun.

French dressing Greek alphabet Siamese cat

Capitalize every word in the **names of people and pets.**

Thomas **A**lva **E**dison **J**ohn **F.** **K**ennedy **S**ylvester

Capitalize a **personal title used with a person's name.**

Dr. May L. Morgan **M**rs. Rivera **G**eneral Colin Powell

Capitalize the following titles when used before names, or when used alone to refer to the current holders of the positions.

the **P**resident (of the United States) **Q**ueen Elizabeth II
the **V**ice-**P**resident (of the United States) the **P**ope

Capitalize the pronoun *I*.

Benjamin and **I** went to the theater.

Using Capital Letters Correctly Capitalize the proper nouns and proper adjectives in the following sentences.

1. Why did auntie em scold dorothy and her mischievous dog named toto?

____

2. My younger brother likes to read books by dr. seuss and maurice sendak.

____

3. Walt disney created mickey mouse, donald duck, goofy, and pluto.

____

4. A popular TV show of the 1950s featured timmy and his dog lassie.

____

5. The forget-me-not, a flower, was the emblem of king henry IV of england.

____

More Proper Nouns

Capitalize the **names of particular places and things.**

Paris **F**rance **E**urope **E**iffel **T**ower
Central **P**ark **B**rooklyn **B**ridge **F**ifth **A**venue

Capitalize the **names of months, days, holidays, and historical events.**

October **S**unday **H**alloween **C**ivil **W**ar

Capitalize the **names of races, religions, nationalities, and languages.**

Native **A**mericans **I**slam **S**paniards **C**hinese

Capitalize **words referring to God and to religious scriptures.**

the **L**ord the **B**ible **J**ehovah the **K**oran

Capitalize the **names of clubs, organizations, and business firms.**

American **K**ennel **C**lub **A**nticruelty **S**ociety **A**pple, **I**nc.

Using Capital Letters Correctly Capitalize the proper nouns and proper adjectives in the following sentences.

1. The boy scouts of america held a food drive for the flood victims.

____

2. An exhibit of african art was shown at the cranbrook academy of art.

____

3. The muslims follow the teachings of mohammed.

____

4. The ancient greeks built the parthenon, a temple in the city of athens.

____

5. The italian artist michelangelo painted scenes from the bible on the ceiling of the sistine chapel.

____

6. During world war II, the united states dropped atomic bombs on two japanese cities.

____

7. Anna jarvis of grafton, west virginia, started a campaign to observe mother's day on the second sunday in may.

____

8. After the earthquake, the red cross offered help to homeless mexicans.

____

First Words

Capitalize the **first word of every sentence.**

What time does the program begin? **W**atch out!

Capitalize the **first word in some lines of poetry.**

Brown and furry
Caterpillar in a hurry
Take your walk
To the shady leaf or stalk.
From "The Caterpillar" by Christina Georgina Rossetti

Sometimes, especially in modern poetry, the poet does not always begin each line with a capital letter.

You Whose Day It Is

You whose day it is,
make it beautiful.
Get out your rainbow,
make it beautiful.
Poem of the Nootka people

Using Capital Letters Correctly Use capital letters where necessary.

Example ~~w~~W hat happens when you rub a balloon against your hair?

1. there was ease in Casey's manner as he stepped into his place,
there was pride in Casey's bearing, and a smile on Casey's face,
and when, responding to the cheers, he lightly doffed his hat,
no stranger in the crowd could doubt 'twas Casey at the bat.
From "Casey at the Bat" by Ernest Lawrence Thayer

2. be seated. court is now in session.

3. scientists predict there will be a major earthquake in california before the end of the century.

4. the atlanta symphony is playing a waltz by johann strauss.

5. hold on tight! the roller coaster is about to go through a tunnel.

6. order your tickets today. hurry! we're almost sold out.

7. when will the eclipse begin?

8. the george washington bridge crosses the hudson river.

Outlines and Titles

Capitalize the **first word of each line of an outline.**

Native Americans of the Great Plains

I. **N**ames of nations
  A. **B**lackfoot
  B. **C**heyenne
  C. **C**row

II. **K**inds of dwellings
  A. **T**epee
  B. **E**arth lodge

Capitalize the **first and last words of a title and all other words** except articles, coordinating conjunctions, and prepositions of four or fewer letters.

The **I**sland of the **B**lue **D**olphins (book)
"**B**allad of the **M**orning **S**treets" (poem)

Using Capital Letters Correctly Use capital letters where necessary.

Example "child on top of a greenhouse" (poem) [corrected: C, T, G]

1. *the peaceable kingdom* (painting)

2. "we are the world" (song)

3. "the secret life of walter mitty" (short story)

4. *pets of the world* (magazine)

5. *where the wild things are* (book)

6. "the river is a piece of the sky" (poem)

7. declaration of independence (document)

8. "the adventure of the speckled band" (short story)

9. *the greatest monsters in the world* (book)

10. native americans of the northeast
  I. cultural groups
    A. lake nations
    B. woodland nations
  II. important foods
    A. lake nations
      1. wild rice
      2. fish and shellfish
    B. woodland nations
      1. corn, squash, and beans
      2. deer and other game

Linking Mechanics and Writing: Capitalization

Imagine that you are a travel agent for a tour company. Plan a two-week vacation for a group of sixth graders. Your group can travel anywhere in the world. Make a list of dates, places, and interesting sights for your group to see. Also, include the name and address of each hotel where your group will stay, the name of two restaurants where the group will eat, and the type of food served in each restaurant.

Additional Practice: Capitalization

Using Capital Letters Correctly Use capital letters where necessary in the following sentences.

1. barbara jordan was born in houston, texas.

2. the main offices of the national football league are located in new york.

3. the name *michigan* comes from chippewa words meaning "great water."

4. this festival of lights is a swedish holiday.

5. In 1541 the spanish explorer coronado traveled in search of gold.

6. the gobi desert lies northwest of beijing, china.

7. Canadians celebrate thanksgiving on october 10.

8. the painting *wealth of 1849* shows miners panning for gold during the california gold rush.

9. George washington did not want the white house to look like a king's palace.

10. the english author a. a. milne created stories featuring a bear named winnie-the-pooh and his friend piglet.

11. television programs
- I. shows about animals
  - A. *nature*
  - B. *wild america*
- II. game shows
  - A. *wheel of fortune*
  - B. *jeopardy!*

12. once upon a midnight dreary, while I pondered, weak and weary,
over many a quaint and curious volume of forgotten lore—
while I nodded, nearly napping, suddenly there came a tapping,
as of someone gently rapping, rapping at my chamber door.

From "The Raven" by Edgar Allan Poe

Review: Capitalization

Using Capital Letters Correctly Use capital letters where necessary.

1. benton harbor is located on the eastern shore of lake michigan.

2. in some parts of ireland, street signs are written in the gaelic language.

3. the mason-dixon line between maryland and pennsylvania divides the north from the south.

4. the koran, the sacred book of islam, is written in arabic.

5. in france, bastille day is like our fourth of july.

6. the gideon society places bibles in hotel rooms.

7. Tarzan, jane, and a chimpanzee named cheeta lived in the jungles of africa.

8. Be sure to visit the san diego zoo when you travel west.

9. "i never saw a moor" is a poem by emily dickinson.

10. Mark twain piloted a riverboat and wrote about his experiences in the book *life on the mississippi.*

11. the peanut butter story
    I. history of peanuts
        A. in the inca civilization
        B. in west africa
    II. manufacturing peanut butter
        A. preparing the peanuts
            1. shelling, sorting, and roasting
            2. removing skin and splitting nuts
        B. grinding and adding other ingredients

12. i'll tell you how the sun rose,
a ribbon at a time.
the steeples swam in amethyst,
the news like squirrels ran.

From "I'll Tell You How the Sun Rose" by Emily Dickinson

The Period

Use a period at the end of declarative sentences and most imperative sentences.

I'll be home right after practice.   Please sit down.

Use a period after an abbreviation or an initial.

A.M.   P.M.   U.S.A.   Dr.   J. P. Morgan

Use a period after each number or letter in an outline and after each number in a list.

Camp Activities

I. Outdoor activities
  A. Canoeing
  B. Archery
  C. Swimming
    1. Lake
    2. Pool

Camping Supplies

1. Pup tent
2. Sleeping bag
3. Mess kit
4. First-aid kit

Using Periods Correctly Add periods where needed.

1. Memorials to Visit in Washington, DC

1 Jefferson Memorial
2 Lincoln Memorial
3 Vietnam Veterans Memorial

2. Mount Vernon, George Washington's home, is about 15 mi south of the nation's capital

3. The Washington Redskins play at Robert F Kennedy Stadium

4. Tourists can visit certain rooms in the White House between 10:00 AM and noon on Tues through Sat

5. The East Room is 79 ft long and about 36 ft wide

6. On Aug 24, 1814, President and Mrs Madison fled from approaching British troops, who set the White House on fire

7. Cultural Attractions in Washington, DC

I Museums
  A National Air and Space Museum
  B Museum of African Art
II Libraries
  A Folger Shakespeare Library
  B Martin Luther King Memorial Library

8. The Smithsonian Institution displays valuable objects from US history

The Question Mark and the Exclamation Point

Use a question mark at the end of an interrogative sentence.

What is the tallest skyscraper? When do geese migrate?

Use an exclamation point at the end of an exclamatory sentence or an imperative sentence that shows strong feeling.

What a great catch that was! Watch out!

Use an exclamation point after an interjection.

Ouch! Wow! Oh, no!

Using Question Marks and Exclamation Points Add needed periods, question marks, and exclamation points. Try not to overuse exclamation points.

1. Hold on tight The boat is starting to rock
2. Wow The fireworks on the Fourth of July are spectacular
3. Good grief Where is Snoopy hiding
4. Hurry Order your tickets today, before it's too late
5. How do dolphins communicate
6. Where were the first telescopes made
7. Unbelievable That strange fish blinks off and on like a flashlight
8. Oh, no A tiger escaped from the circus and is roaming the city streets
9. Jacques Cousteau suffered from health problems as a young boy, but he still learned to swim well
10. Long ago, didn't some people believe that the movements of a giant animal caused earthquakes
11. Great Your routine on the balance beam was nearly perfect
12. Will space travel someday be possible for people other than astronauts
13. Incredible A spaceship just landed in the schoolyard
14. What kinds of shells can you find on the beach
15. Look out A deer is standing in the middle of the road

Commas That Separate Ideas

Use commas to separate three or more items in a series. Place a comma after each item in the series except the last.

> A singer, a magician, and a dancer were in the talent show.
> Anne dressed quickly, grabbed a muffin, and headed for the bus.

Use a comma when you use *and, but,* or *or* to combine two sentences. Put a comma before the conjunction.

> The clock chimed the hour, and we all shouted "Happy New Year!"
> Do you want to play soccer, or shall we stay in and listen to music?

Use a comma whenever the reader might be confused.

> In the morning light streams in through my window.
> In the morning, light streams in through my window.

> After I left the dog stopped barking.
> After I left, the dog stopped barking.

Using Commas Correctly Place commas wherever they are needed.

1. Brown paper bags leotards and chocolate chip cookies are all creations of women inventors.
2. In the story books were forbidden.
3. To make candles, you will need wax old crayons and cotton wicks.
4. Hank Monk drove a stagecoach mined for gold and rode for the pony express.
5. The Amish people lead simple lives and they have strong religious beliefs.
6. In the 1940s, Preston Tucker designed a car that was safe comfortable and relatively inexpensive.
7. Dark clouds moved across the sky and soon afterward the rainstorm began.
8. Michelle changed the tire oiled the chain and tightened the brake.
9. Suddenly the door of the house flew open and a gust of wind knocked over a lamp.
10. A girl a pig and a spider are the main characters in *Charlotte's Web.*
11. Outlaws in the Wild West robbed banks trains and stagecoaches.
12. You have more than 200 bones inside your body and many of them are like stiff tubes.
13. The dog chased the cat over the fence across the street and up the tree.
14. Dorothy travels to Emerald City with the Scarecrow the Tin Woodman and the Cowardly Lion.
15. The electric eel is a fascinating creature but it can produce a deadly shock.

Commas That Set Off Special Elements

Use a comma after *yes, no,* or *well* at the beginning of a sentence.

Yes, I saw her there.   Well, I may be late.

Use commas to set off the name of a person spoken to.

Please come inside, Jimmy.
Mark, may I borrow your book?
I think, Joan, that you have my keys.

Use commas to set off an appositive. An **appositive** follows a noun and renames the noun.

Our mail carrier, Ms. Valdez, is never sick.

Use a comma to separate the parts of a date. Use a comma after the last part of a date in the middle of a sentence.

My sister was born on December 15, 1979.
On August 26, 1920, women in the United States won the right to vote.

Use a comma to separate the name of a city from the name of a state or country. If the two names come in the middle of a sentence, place a comma after the second name too.

In Philadelphia, Pennsylvania, the Declaration of Independence was signed.
My aunt and uncle came from Sydney, Australia.

Using Commas Correctly Add commas where needed.

1. On April 15 1912 the *Titanic* sank in the Atlantic Ocean.
2. Gwendolyn Brooks a poet was born in 1917.
3. Yes Daryl I agree that our town should build a recycling center.
4. The *Bounty* sailed to Tahiti an island in the South Pacific.
5. The Wright brothers flew their airplane near Kitty Hawk North Carolina.
6. Lewis Carroll the author of *Alice's Adventures in Wonderland* also taught mathematics.
7. The ballet *Sleeping Beauty* opens on Friday September 11.
8. Over 10 million visitors a year flock to Disneyland in Anaheim California.
9. Let's make a mural to celebrate Earth Day Sylvia.
10. Angela did you know that the *Guinness Book of Records* lists the largest yo-yo ever made?

Other Uses for Commas

Use a comma to set off the explanatory words of a direct quotation.

Connie answered**,** "Four people were absent."

"The track meet begins at three**,**" replied Ann.

"After the game**,**" said Tony**,** "we will meet at my house."

Use a comma after the greeting of a friendly letter and after the closing of any letter.

Dear Karen**,**　　Respectfully yours**,**　　Your friend**,**

Using Commas Correctly Add commas wherever they are needed.

1. The judge pounded his gavel and said "Order in the court!"

2. "Everyone in this mansion" said the detective "is a suspect."

3. Paul Revere shouted to the colonists "The British are coming!"

4. "Swing your partners round and round" yelled the caller at the square dance.

5. Lin asked "What is the largest baseball stadium in the United States?"

6. Kevin wondered "Was Johnny Appleseed a real person?"

7. "One of the witnesses" said the lawyer "is not telling the truth."

8. The space explorers told reporters "Mars is our next destination."

9. "Many children in our city" said the social worker "are homeless."

10. The spy announced "I have cracked the secret code."

11. "Please call me" said Marva "when the Grammy Awards begin."

12. The sea captain bellowed "Drop anchor!"

13. Dear Julio

14. Your friend
Emily

15. Sincerely yours
Lester

The Apostrophe

Use an apostrophe to show possession. To form the possessive of a singular noun, add an apostrophe and *s.*

baby + 's = baby's   James + 's = James's

To form the possessive of a plural noun that ends in *s,* add only an apostrophe.

babies + ' = babies'

To form the possessive of a plural noun that does not end in *s,* add an apostrophe and *s.*

children + 's = children's   deer + 's = deer's

Use an apostrophe in a contraction. A **contraction** is made by joining two words and omitting one or more letters. An apostrophe replaces the missing letters.

it + is = it's   are + not = aren't
who + is = who's   you + will = you'll

Using Apostrophes Correctly On the blank, write the possessive form of the italicized word.

1. *friends* party ______________
2. *today* news ______________
3. *mice* cages ______________
4. *members* dues ______________
5. *Ross* treehouse ______________
6. *sister* room ______________
7. *men* shoes ______________
8. *student* report ______________
9. *pitcher* fastball ______________
10. *fox* cleverness ______________

Writing Contractions Correctly Write each of the following word combinations as a contraction.

1. does not ______________
2. she would ______________
3. they are ______________
4. must not ______________
5. would not ______________
6. it is ______________
7. has not ______________
8. do not ______________
9. I will ______________
10. is not ______________

The Hyphen

Use a hyphen after the first part of a word at the end of a line. Then write the second part on the next line.

> The sun disappeared as dark clouds were begin-
> ning to fill the sky.

Never divide a word that has only one syllable, such as *chief.* Do not write a single letter at the end or beginning of a line. A dictionary shows how to divide a word into syllables.

Use a hyphen in compound numbers from twenty-one through ninety-nine and in fractions.

forty-two carloads   forty-ninth state   one-half of the pizza

Using Hyphens Correctly Divide each of the following words. Write the word in two parts as you would at the end of the line. If the word cannot be divided, write *Do Not Divide* on the line. You may use a dictionary to complete this exercise.

Example skateboard

1. cassette ____________	**6.** eclipse ____________
2. stapler ____________	**7.** controls ____________
3. apart ____________	**8.** defense ____________
4. soda ____________	**9.** computer ____________
5. digital ____________	**10.** zero ____________

Using Hyphens in Compound Numbers In the following sentences, add hyphens wherever necessary.

1. Have any professional football players been more than thirty nine years old?
2. A piano has thirty six black keys and fifty two white keys.
3. The rock star donated one third of his salary to charities.
4. Will robots replace factory workers in the twenty first century?
5. California is the home state of about one fourth of all major league baseball players.

Use a colon after the greeting in a business letter.

Dear Madam: Dear Mr. Romero:

Use a colon between numerals representing hours and minutes.

6:00 A.M.   9:55 P.M.

Remember to capitalize the letters and to use periods after each letter in the abbreviations *A.M.* and *P.M.*

There are two ways to combine two related sentences into one. The first way is to use a conjunction, such as *and, but,* or *or,* to connect the sentences. When you combine sentences in this way, use a comma before the conjunction.

Mr. Scott began his lecture, and the students listened attentively.

The second way to combine two related sentences is to use a semicolon. The semicolon takes the place of both the comma and the conjunction.

Mr. Scott began his lecture; the students listened attentively.

Using Colons and Semicolons Correctly Add colons, semicolons, and commas where needed.

July 4 19—

Dear Mr. Grant

Our puppet theater in Tyler Texas will present the story "Cinderella" this weekend. Please print the schedule in the Tuesday paper. The play will be performed on Saturday July 9 at 1100 A.M. and 300 P.M. it will also be performed on Sunday July 10 at 1030 A.M. 230 P.M. and 700 P.M.

Sincerely yours
Toy Chest
Puppet Theater

Using Semicolons to Join Sentences Correct each run-on sentence by inserting a semicolon where it is needed.

1. Yellow jackets are a kind of wasp their smooth brown bodies are marked with yellow stripes.
2. The pickup truck roared down the dirt road huge clouds of dust trailed behind it.
3. The Venus' flytrap is an unusual plant it eats insects.
4. A tiny car stops in the middle of the circus ring a crowd of clowns pop out of the car.
5. Hugo was shot from a cannon he sailed across the circus tent and landed in a small net.

Quotation Marks

When you write what a person has said, you are writing a **quotation.** A **direct quotation** is a restatement of the person's exact words. If you do not write the exact words, you are writing an **indirect quotation.**

Put quotation marks before and after the words of a direct quotation.

> **"**Don't feed the animals,**"** warned the zoo keeper.

Separate the words of a direct quotation from the rest of the sentence with a comma or an end mark in addition to quotation marks. Capitalize the first word of a direct quotation that is a sentence.

> Julie exclaimed**, "T**he band is marching!**"**
> **"T**he band is marching**!"** Julie exclaimed.

Place a question mark or an exclamation point inside quotation marks if it belongs to the quotation itself.

> Michael asked, "Did the bird's wing heal**?**"
> "It's perfect**!**" answered Marianne.

Place a question mark or an exclamation point outside quotation marks if it does not belong to the quotation.

> Did Dad say, "Come home at seven o'clock"**?**
> I was shocked to hear her say, "I'll go"**!**

Using Quotation Marks Add quotation marks and other punctuation where necessary. Write *C* for *Correct* if no additional punctuation is needed.

1. Give me King Midas said the power to turn everything I touch into gold.
2. The deputy told the sheriff A stranger wearing a black hat just rode into town.
3. Rumpelstiltskin asked What is my name?
4. Please welcome Michael Jackson said the talk-show host.
5. Cinderella's wicked stepsisters told her that she was too dirty to go to the ball.
6. Tin soldier said the goblin don't wish for what does not belong to you.
7. Mayor, how will the new major league ballpark affect the city? asked the reporter.
8. Merlin told Arthur that he should draw the sword from the stone.
9. The next song said the disc jockey is dedicated to all the students at Truman Middle School.
10. Be careful warned the radio announcer Freezing rains have made the roads very icy.

Punctuating Titles

Put quotation marks around the titles of stories, poems, reports, articles, and chapters of a book.

"Spring Song" (poem)   "The Ransom of Red Chief" (story)

Underline the title of a book, magazine, play, motion picture, or TV series. In print, these titles appear in italics.

<u>Mary Jane</u> by Dorothy Sterling   *Mary Jane* by Dorothy Sterling

Underline the title of a painting or the name of a ship.

<u>Washington Crossing the Delaware</u> (painting)
<u>Queen Elizabeth II</u> (ship)

Punctuating Titles Add the necessary quotation marks or underlining for the following titles.

1. Raymond's Run (story)
2. The Night the Bed Fell (article)
3. Cricket (magazine)
4. The Blob (movie)
5. The Adventures of Tom Sawyer (book)
6. Nature (TV series)
7. The Scream (painting)
8. The Miracle Worker (play)
9. The Moon and Beyond (chapter)
10. Macavity: The Mystery Cat (poem)

Punctuating Titles in Sentences Add the necessary quotation marks or underlining for the titles in the following sentences.

1. I found Poe's story The Cask of Amontillado in the book Tales of Terror.
2. At the library Carla checked out a print of Van Gogh's painting Sunflowers.
3. The article The Enduring Rock appeared in National Geographic magazine.
4. Henry Hudson sailed across the Atlantic in the Half Moon.
5. The title of Lorraine Hansberry's play A Raisin in the Sun is taken from a line in Langston Hughes's poem Harlem.

Linking Mechanics and Writing: Punctuation

Imagine that you are a talk-show host. You have just interviewed a very interesting guest. Who was this person? What questions did you ask him or her? What were the person's answers? Write the conversation between you and your guest. Remember to use correct punctuation for direct quotations.

Additional Practice: Punctuation

Using Punctuation Correctly in Letters Add punctuation as needed in the following letter.

209 Lake Road
Missouri City Texas 77459
Jan 8 19—

McGurk Publishing Company
7000 Hollister Road
Cleveland Heights Ohio 44118

Dear Sir or Madam

Would you please tell me where I can write Nora Cruz the author of Thirty six Adventures I enjoyed the book very much I especially liked the escape from the tower, when Adelaide cried Wait Conrad I dont know how to fly

I would like to tell the author how much I admire the book Im looking forward to reading her story Six Hours till Venus in the next issue of Analog

Yours truly
Raji A Chandra

Punctuating Sentences Correctly Punctuate the following sentences correctly, using the punctuation marks you have studied.

1. On July 10 1890 Wyoming became the forty fourth state
2. Rosie the Riveter wore overalls carried a lunch pail and worked in a factory
3. Did you know that during World War II many women built planes ships and weapons
4. Samuel Wilson the original Uncle Sam was born on September 13 1766 in Arlington Massachusetts
5. Bumblebees make their nests underground but honeybees build their hives in hollow trees
6. Wow exclaimed Carmen The rock concert at the Rosemont Horizon was awesome
7. Dr Charles R Drew an African-American physician set up blood banks during World War II Drews efforts helped save millions of lives
8. Kinds of Dogs

   1 Hounds   3 Terriers

   2 Toy dogs   4 Wild dogs
9. Watch out Rita Youre heading toward a sharp rock
10. Have you read T S Eliots book titled Old Possum's Book of Practical Cats

Review: Punctuation

Punctuating Sentences Correctly Punctuate the following sentences correctly, using the punctuation marks you have studied.

1. Kim asked Have you seen Babes in Toyland a funny movie starring Laurel and Hardy
2. Hispanic Americans make up about one tenth of the total US population
3. After Margo ate the squirrels gathered the crumbs
4. Many of James Thurbers stories essays and cartoons appeared in The New Yorker a well-known magazine
5. The scientist screamed Oh no What have I done Ive created a terrible monster
6. A hungry fox wanted to eat ripe clusters of grapes hanging from a vine but he couldnt reach them
7. Yes the rumba the cha-cha and the mambo are popular Cuban dances
8. These are my favorite authors of childrens books:
   1 E B White
   2 A A Milne
   3 Dr Seuss
9. The Civil War began on April 12 1861 four years of bloody battles followed
10. Were number one shouted the football players in the mens locker room

Punctuating a Letter Correctly Add punctuation where needed in the following letter.

April 12 19—

Dear Mrs Walker

Were glad that you and your class will visit the science museum in San Diego California. The museum opens at 930 AM. The laser show begins at 1000 AM A film about energy shown in the audi torium at 1130 is about twenty five minutes long.

Well see you on Thursday May 3. Please call me if you have any questions.

Sincerely yours
Victor Chung

Directions One or more of the underlined sections in the following sentences may contain an error in grammar, usage, punctuation, spelling, or capitalization. Write the letter of each incorrect section. Then rewrite the section correctly. If there is no error in an item, write *D.*

Example Benjamin asked me "What (A) are the three colors of the mexican (B) flag?" (C) No error (D)

Answer A—me, "What
B—Mexican

1. The policeman shouted "Fire"! (A) Fortunately, everyone got out of the building quickly, and (B) no one was hurt. (C) No error (D)

2. On December 17, 1903, (A) near Kitty Hawk, North Carolina, the Wright brothers flew thier (B) airplane for the first time and (C) a new age began. No error (D)

3. "Dont (A) one of you fire," said William Prescott "until (B) you see the whites of their eyes." He gave this order at Bunker Hill during the American Revolution. (C) No error (D)

4. Well the (A) mail comes in at 11:30 AM (B) today, but (C) it won't be sorted until an hour later. No error (D)

5. When Yoki visits the Canadian city (A) of Montreal, Quebec, she plans to practice her french. (B) About two thirds (C) of the people there speak that language. No error (C)

6. The second sunday (A) in May (B) is Mother's day. (C) No error (D)

7. Have you read Lewis Carroll's poem "The (A) Walrus and the Carpenter?" (B) My grandpa (C) used to read it to me. No error (D)

8. Every year, Mardi Gras is celebrated in New Orleans and other cities in
A
the south. A lively, colorful festival takes place before Easter. No error
B C D

9. There is a proverb about boasting that states, "the empty vessel makes
A B
the greatest sound." No error
C D

10. Steves' father, a veterinarian, will speak to our class today. Were
A B C
bringing our pets. No error
D

11. Starting at 7:30 A.M. every day, my favorite radio station plays country
A B
music, rock and golden oldies. No error
C D

12. Now I'd like to read Jack London's *The Call of the Wild* or maybe a
A B C
book of his short stories. No error
D

13. Before you leave the campfire should be completely doused with water.
A
The woods this summer are much drier than usual. No error
B C D

14. Which do you think is longest, the Mississippi river or the Nile?
A B C
No error
D

15. As far as we know, Dr. Joy Allen and Rabbi David Friedman will both
A B
be speaking at the Fisher Auditorium tonight. No error
C D

Proofreading Practice: Understanding Sentences

A. Writing Sentences Correctly Read the following announcement. Then use proofreading marks to correct all errors in capitalization, punctuation, spelling, and grammar. Look especially for sentence fragments and run-on sentences. Add words to make fragments complete sentences.

Is your car so dirty that people write "Wash me" in its dirt are the seats and floor of your car covered with food rappers, leafs, and newspapers? A good wash and interior cleaning may be just what your car needs. The sixth-grade students of Pleasant Valley middle School invite you to a carwash at 734 w. Reba Street on Saturday, september 25, between the hours of 9:00 A.M. and 5:00 P.M. Our to expert teams will give your car the special treatment it deserves. Our first team will scrub and buff the exterior of your car to a sparkleing shine. will clear out all of the interior trash and vacuum your seats and floor. The exterior wash and buff polish will cost $3.00. The interior cleaning will $2.00. will donate all proceeds to friendship house, a shelter for the homeless.

B. Writing More Sentences Correctly Read the following news article. Then correct all the errors. You may need to add words to make fragments complete sentences.

The sixth-grade students at Pleasant Valley Middle School recently put good citizenship into action. wanted to do there part in helping to feed our citys many homeless poeple. On saturday, September 25, this fine group of students washed cars in their school's parking lot to raise money for Friendship House on Bridgeport avenue. Fortunately, the project. The students earned a whopping $175!

Mrs abernathy, the director of Friendship House, expressed her gratitude to the students. has invited them to visit the shelter and learn about its services to the community these young people at Pleasant Valley Middle School have certainly set a good example of community spirit for us all.

Proofreading Practice: Understanding Nouns

Using Nouns Correctly Read the business letter below. Then use proofreading marks to correct all errors in capitalization, punctuation, spelling, and grammar. Pay special attention to the use of nouns.

709 Mason street

Ashley, Pennsylvania 18062

November 14, 19—

Dear Mr Farrell:

I am eleven years old. My dad and stepmom showed me your column in yesterday's Daily herald newspaper. They explained that you are a restaurant critic. You pick a restaurant to eat at and then you tell your readers what is good or bad about it.

I am writing because I have a favor to ask of you. In your column, could you talk about the childrens menues in this citys restaurants? Those menus do not give us kids enough choices! We do not like only hamburgers, hot dogs, grilled cheese sandwichs, and spaghetti! I often don't want any of those things when I eat out, so I order from the adult menu items on that menu are more expensive, and the portions are too large. I can't eat that much food, and Im tired of carrying home those doggie bags!

Please tell restaurant owners that kids also like lasagna, pizza, pork chops, shrimps, chicken, and tacoes. Can't these appear on their childrens's menus? Also please tell them that kids should be able to order a childs portion of potatos, salad, and soup to. I'm sure that familys all over the city would like to see these changes. It would save them money, and less food would go to waste.

Yours truly

Reggie Roberts

P.S. My dad and stepmom took me to the Knifes and Forks restaurant after you recommended it. The small loafs of warm bread that came with our salads were awesome! We enjoyed the singing waiters and waitressess too.

Proofreading Practice: Understanding Verbs

Using Verbs Correctly Read the passage below. Then use proofreading marks to correct all errors in capitalization, punctuation, spelling, and grammar. Pay special attention to the use of verbs.

Southwest of Colorado Springs, Colorado, lays an old gold-mining town that is not known to many americans today. Cripple Creek is just a tourist attraction now, but it once was the world's largest gold-producing area.

Visitors ride the train that runs to Anaconda and back. It makes stops, and the conductor tells exciting tails about the history of the area. Listeners here how Cripple Creek got its name. As the story goes, an early settler's son was working on a house that he and his father were building. Before the boy knew what had happened, he had fell off of the house and broke a leg. On the same day, a calf broke its leg while jumping over a stream. The settler was heard to say, "This sure is a cripple creek."

The conductor explains that Cripple Creek was once just a cow pasture. Then the cowpoke and rancher Bob Womack striked gold in 1891, and Americas last major gold rush began settlers came from all over the country in search of fortunes.

The conductor also tells about the fire that broke out in 1896. He says that a second fire broke out only five days later. Cripple Creek was completely destroyed, but listeners smile again when they hear how the townspeople didn't set back and give up in the face of disaster. They rebiult the town in brick and many of those buildings stil stand passengers raise in their seats as the conductor points to an opera house, a school, and a hotel. He adds that Cripple Creek reached its peak in 1900. By then, its population had growed to 35,000, and there were 30 millionaires.

"The Cripple Creek area produced more than $600 million in gold during its boom days," the conductor says, "and the gold isnt gone. Some local miners say that 80 percent of the gold in the area is still untapped." The train starts moving once again. The whistle blows. The passengers know that they have came to the end of the line as they see the Cripple creek station just ahead.

Proofreading Practice: Understanding Pronouns

Using Pronouns Correctly Read the passage below. Then use proofreading marks to correct all errors in capitalization, punctuation, spelling, and grammar. Pay special attention to the use of pronouns.

Little did I know when I woke up this morning that Amy and I would be travelling through time. Dad had told we kids never to touch anything in his laboratory but our curiosity got the best of us this time. Amy and me saw the time machine with all of it's buttons and knobs, and we thought it was a giant video game. We were drawn to the machine like magnets! Her and me darted over to the front panel and started wildly pushing the buttons and knobs to see what would happen. A series of blurry images began to shoot across the screen above us. Then I pushed a lever at my side of the panel and a window next to the lever displayed a month, day, and year. It was may 5 2056! Suddenly, the laboratory disapeared, and amy and I found ourselves on a street lined with towering dome-shaped buildings. We were pretty scared, but both of us did his best to remain calm.

"Great! What do we do now." Amy asked nervously.

"Let's take a look around," I suggested.

Amy and I walked across the street toward a building that a steady stream of people were entering and leaveing. The sign out front said Fast Refueling.

"It must be some kind of gasoline station, Amy said.

She and me walked into the building and saw three large symbols on the back wall. In front of each symbol was a long line of people. each person would take a turn lying their hands flat against a glowing bulb sticking partly out of the wall. After about ten seconds, the person would turn and leave. Many of the people seemed to be awaiting his or her turn eagerly.

The words of a man behind a counter at our left made Amy and I jump back in surprize. "May I take you're order?" he asked.

Proofreading Practice: Understanding Adjectives

Using Adjectives Correctly Read this interview between a reporter and a professional football player. Then use proofreading marks to correct all errors in capitalization, punctuation, spelling, and grammar. Pay attention to the use of adjectives.

Question: The name Carter Utah is a interesting one. Is Utah your real last name?

Answer: Utah has been shortened from Utahowitz. Utah is the easiest of the two names for people to say and write.

Question: What is it like to be a quarterback for the morgan mammoths?

Answer: It has been the most big thrill of my life. Professional football is a tough sport though. I have to practice hard and exercise frequently.

Question: What was your most memorable game and what made it so memorable?

Answer: I'll never forget the game between the Mammoths and the Cougars in 1991. I threw a 40-yard pass that was caught for the winning touchdown in the last seconds of the final quarter. Them fans went wild! I was a hero after that there game.

Question: What is the greater number of times you have been tackled in one game?

Answer: I was tackled six times in the Fenwick game. Our best linemen were out, and the substitute linemen didn't protect me very good.

Question: Which team's defense is the most toughest of all to pass against?

Answer: The Welby Colts are extremly tough. they use a tricky zone defense.

Question: Which opposing linebacker gives you the mostest trouble?

Answer: Fenwick's Brian Majors comes at me like a wrecking ball! He's more bigger, more quicker, and more stronger than any other linebacker I know.

Question: What is the worsest injury you have ever recieved during a game?

Answer: Once I suffered a separated collarbone and was out for six weeks.

Question: What advice can you give kids who want to be professional athletes.

Answer: Practice often and work hard. Also, try to get tips for improveing your game from players who are more skillfuler than you.

Proofreading Practice: Understanding Adverbs

Using Adverbs Correctly Read the story below. Then use proofreading marks to correct all errors in capitalization, punctuation, spelling, and grammar. Pay special attention to the use of adverbs.

I got a queasy feeling in my stumik when Mom and Dad told me they had volunteered to host this year's family reunion. I immediatly had flashbacks to past partys at our house that had turned into disasters. At last summers barbecue, a sudden downpour had forced our fifty guests to stand elbow to elbow in the garage while eating soggy hamburgers and potato salad. At my sister mia's birthday party, the clown had canceled his performance after tripping on a toy and spraining his back. I wondered what new disaster might be waiting to happen at this years family reunion.

All of the relatives agreed that a potluck dinner would be the less amount of work for Mom. They planned to bring the dishes they liked best Mom, Dad, and I worked more harder than ever before to get the house ready.

On the day of the reunion, the mood was quite merrily. Relatives arrived with mouthwatering tempting dishes. They arranged there dishs careful on the dining-room table. Then everyone claped and cheered as Dad proudly entered the room with a platter that held a large smoked salmon. It looked real well. After sitting the platter in the center of the table, Dad took a long bow. I remember looking over my shoulder at that moment and seeing Mia opening the front door to let in our dog, Ralph.

"No Mia! Don't let him in! I shouted, but my warning came to late. Ralph charged straight for the table jumped, and landed ungraceful on the near end. The force of his landing caused both him and the tablecloth to slide fast. Dishes flew in all directions, and to make matters worser, Ralph managed somehow to grab a big mouthful of the smoked salmon before dad caught him at the far end of the table. Dad scolded Ralph for behaving so bad and pulled him out of the room by his collar. Relatives groaned as they surveyed the damage. Mom didn't look at all good. I remember shaking my head and thinking, "heres one more party disaster to add to the list."

Proofreading Practice: Prepositions and Conjunctions

A. Using Prepositions and Conjunctions Correctly Read the student opinion statement below. Then use proofreading marks to correct all errors in capitalization, punctuation, spelling, and grammar. Pay special attention to the use of prepositions and conjunctions.

I am completly in favor of the decision that the first week in november be Courtesy Week at Westchester junior high school. Its about time that all of we students start treating one another with more respect. Rudeness is getting out of control in our school, and name-calling, especially between the older students, has become an ordinary occurence. Even basic expressions of common courtesy, such as "please," "thank you," and "excuse me," to often go unspoken. Maybe if we were all more polite, there would be fewer arguments and misunderstandings in and around our school. Courtesy Week can be a time for you and I to be reminded of the many ways in which we should show respect and consideration for one another. If we all work together, we can bring back the pleasant environment that once filled the halls and classrooms of Westchester Junior High. After all, courtesy takes very little effort but the rewards can be great!

B. Using More Prepositions and Conjunctions Correctly Read the Courtesy Week slogans below. Then correct all errors.

This is courtesy week. please participate.

It feels well to be nice.

Courtesy starts with you and I.

Remember the golden rule: Do unto others as you would have them do unto you.

Give compliments, not insults.

Show you care. Say "Im sorry."

Courtesy is contagious. Help it spred

Do it write. Be polite.

Proofreading Practice: Subject-Verb Agreement

Using Subjects and Verbs Correctly Read the report below. Then use proofreading marks to correct all errors in capitalization, punctuation, spelling, and grammar. Look especially for sentences in which subjects and verbs do not agree.

"Face of Elvis Seen on Surface of Moon!" "Titanic Passenger found Alive!" "Farmer Traps 23-Pound Grasshopper!" Unbeleivable headlines like these appear on the front pages of tabloid newspapers. The stories that follow these headlines are just as incredible, yet millions of tabloids are sold every day. Why do so many people buy them.

One reason for the success of the tabloids is their content. Everyone like reading about amazing events and the tabloids are cashing in on that fact. Men, women, and children has been entertained by amazing stories for hundreds of years. Even before such stories was wrote down, they was shared orally. In fact, the themes that made good stories then make good stories today. For example, the old theme of the hero who didnt die has been repeated over and over again in the stories about Elvis sightings. A fascination with monsters makes stories about Bigfoot popular. Other stories of long ago tells about princes and princesses who live happily ever after. The prince and princess stories in modern tabloids are about hollywood celebritys and political figures, but these characters often do not live happily ever after.

Another reason for the success of the tabloids are the method used to market them. Shoppers can easily pick up one or more tabloids as they pass threw the checkout line at the supermarket. The bold headlines seems to shout at shoppers as they stand and wait there turn. Some individuals just sniker as their eyes pass from one sensational headline to the next. There is others who cannot resist the urge to read more than just the headlines. Those individuals can be seen tossing one or more newspapers into their shopping carts.

Does readers believe what they read in the tabloids? it is probably safe to say that most readers read tabloid newspapers not to become better informed but to be entertained.

Proofreading Practice: Capitalization

Capitalizing Words Correctly Read the letter below. Then use proofreading marks to correct all errors in capitalization, punctuation, spelling, and grammar. Pay special attention to the use of capital letters.

march 15, 19—

Dear madre and padre,

Buenos días! As you can see, this trip to mexico is giving me a chance to practice my spanish. I even spoke some Spanish to the flight attendant on the airplane. When she asked if I wanted a snack, I said "Si. She smiled as she handed me my snack tray.

I'll never forget my first view of the yucatán peninsula from the air. I saw a Tropical Rain Forest in one large area. It made me think of stories I had heard about companys that are clearing away rain forests for mining ranching and timber projects. I wondered how people can destroy such beautiful places. As we neared cancún, I got my first glimpse of the Caribbean sea. Its the clearest, bluest water I've ever seen.

Señorita Estrada and señor González, our chaperones, are making sure that we learn about the History of the peninsula. Yesterday we visited an ancient city called chichén itzá. The city was built by the Mayas, a group of indians who produced wonderful art and architecture. The ruins there are awesome! My favorite was the great pyramid called El castillo, which stands in the center of the main plaza. It has four grand stairways that lead to a Temple at the top. We chose a stairway and climbed all ninety-one steps! The main entrance at the North side of the temple has to serpent colums, and a sanctuary lays behind them.

In a few minutes, we will be going to a mexican fiesta at a restaurant called la casa grande. a mariachi, a strolling band of musicians, will entertain us during dinner. I can hardly wait!

Adios

Camille

Proofreading Practice: Punctuation

Using Punctuation Correctly Read the passage below. Then use proofreading marks to correct all errors in capitalization, punctuation, spelling, and grammar. Pay special attention to the use of punctuation marks.

Imagine a hairy creature creeping closer and closer to its prey. Suddenly, the creature pounces on its unsuspecting victim. The prey is completly devoured.

Does this description sound like a scene from a monster movie. Well you may feel that you are part of a monster movie as you witness similar performances at the Insect Zoo in the Smithsonian Institution's Museum of natural history in Washington, D.C.

A sign at the zoo displays the times for daily tarantula feedings. At 1030 AM, 1130 AM, and 130 PM, a keeper holding a cage steps out of a back room and announces that the feeding will begin. He sets down on a carpet and removes the lid of the cage. Curious bystanders rush over to get a closer look at the tarantula inside.

The keeper may introduce his furry friend by saying, "This is Terror. She lives in the Insect Zoo but she is not an insect. Insects have six legs and three body parts however Terror has eight legs and two body parts. Her fisical features are typical of arachnids, such as spiders scorpions, and ticks. In spite of what you may think, Terrors bite wont kill a human, the keeper continues. "It does hurt a bit, but no more than a bee sting.

The keeper informs the visitors that Terror may not be hungry. Tarantulas are not big eaters" he explains. "they need water, but they can survive for two years without eating. Terror gets fed only once a week here. As the keeper speaks, he drops a cricket into the cage. In the blink of an eye, terror pounces on the cricket and injects venom with her long fangs. "That venom is turning the crickets insides to liquid," explains the keeper "It will take Terror about one half hour to suck out the liquid. Then she will discard the skeleton."

"I can't look" one observer cries out. Others are fascinated by Terror's unusual style of dining and watch closly. Moments later, the crowd begin to scatter the keeper replaces the lid and returns the cage to the back room.